Heart Healthy Smart Recipes

Smart Eating for Heart Health

Table of Contents

Spicy Chicken Wraps

Ants On A Log

Grilled Pineapple Fruit Salad

Fruit 'N Nut Bars

Simple Guacamole

Coconut Shrimp

Avocado Cashew Hummus with Cucumber

Cocoa Date Spread

Cashew Spinach Dip with Bell Pepper

Sweet Carrot Raisin Salad

Fresh Zesty Pico de Gallo

Sardine & Avocado on Endives

Smoked Salmon Bites

Ginger Spice Cookies

Orange Cranberry Muffins

Spinach Mushroom Muffins

Health Conscious Baking

Citrus Herb Anzac Biscuits

Pure Pumpkin Bread

Nutty Apple Crumble

Gingerbread Cookies

Strawberry Toaster Pastry

Cocoa Zucchini Muffin

Sweet Cherry Fig Newtons

Lemon Coconut Pinwheel Cookies

Pineapple Coconut Cake

Sweet Banana Shortbreads

Cranberry Almond Cookies

Walnut Raisin Cookies

Cinnamon Raisin Bread

Avocado Club Muffin

Easy Poppy Seed Muffins

Carrot Cake Cookie Bars

Apple Pastries

Orange Cranberry Muffins

Onion Crumpets

Spinach Mushroom Muffins

Rosemary Basil Scones

Fennel Breakfast Biscuits

Everything Bagels

Avocado Banana Bread

Savory Spiced Pineapple Bread

Citrus Curry Spice Bread

Asian Orange Muffins

Sage Sausage Buns

"Corn" Muffins

Key Lime Coconut Bars

Heart Healthy Lunches

Chicken Soup

Emerald Soup

Indian Egg Fried "Rice"

Easy Mushroom Bites

Veggie Musakhan

Hearty Sweet Hunter Stew

All-Day Meatball Marinara

Thai Coconut Soup

Turkey Bacon Club Salad

Beef and Plantain Stir-Fry

Tuna Spread

Healthy Chicken Pot Pie

Asian Empanada

Stewed Chicken and Dumplings

Kelp Noodle Stir-Fry

Quick Chili

Veggie Burger

Kelp Noodle Salad

Simple Gazpacho + Tortilla Chips

Shrimp Taco

Grain-Free Tortillas

Zucchini Salad with Sundried Tomato Sauce

Spicy Tuna Tartare

Almond Cheese and Nori

Mango Ginger Apple Salad

Raspberry Almond Salad

Smoked Salmon Avocado Salad

Fresh Sashimi Bento Bowl

Spicy Chicken Wraps

Chopped Spicy Zucchini

Uptown Clam Chowder

Heart Healthy Dinners

Cashew Chicken Satay

Orange Chicken

Luscious Zucchini Lasagna

Chickplant Filets

Salmon with Berry Chutney

Mirepoix with Red Sauce

Mushroom Masala

Sweet & Spicy Venison Stir-Fry

Herb Roasted Pork Tenderloin

Ground Beef Stuffed Peppers

Healthy Gyro with Creamy Tzatziki

Chicken Souvlaki Kebobs

Stuffed Cabbage in Tomato Sauce

Slow Cooker Herbed Duck

Jamaican Curried Goat

Basque Style Cod Fish Stew

Indian Lamb Stew

Macadamia Crusted Ahi Tuna

Cashew Crunch Kelp Noodle Salad

Tuna Tartar with Avocado and Mango

Dill Stuffed Tomatoes

Black Pepper Stew

Spicy Kale Quiche

Red Pepper Chicken Fries

Nuts & Turkey Burgers

Chicken Bruschetta

Spicy Zucchini Eggplant Dine

Baked Tilapia Filets

Red Pepper with Chicken Toppings

Natural Italian Chicken Sausage

Why Eat Heart Healthy?

Reduce intake of saturated and trans fats; do 30 minutes of exercise every day; reduce salt and sugar; stop smoking; avoid cholesterol; lose some weight: tips for a healthy heart abound both on the Internet and traditional media. Sometimes, it's hard to differentiate between good and bad advice, especially since we cannot tell the long-term consequences of our lifestyle until many years later.

We all know how important it is to protect our heart. The fist-sized organ relentlessly pumps blood 24 hours a day in order to supply every tissue and organ with a fresh dose of oxygen and nutrients. When the heart struggles, our health shows for it. The consequences of not taking care of our heart can lead to chest pain, stroke and even premature death. Because of this, specialists offer truckloads of advice on taking care of one of our most important organs.

In the past, we were told that all fat is bad for the heart. Later, it was discovered that not all fat is the same. Fats were then divided in multiple categories: saturated, unsaturated, trans, cholesterol and more. We were told to load up on unsaturated fats and avoid the others as much as possible. Lately, new evidence emerged on this topic: saturated fat is no longer the enemy, and neither is cholesterol. In fact, cholesterol is necessary for good health, and medium-chain triglycerides (a type of saturated fat) actually have some beneficial properties against heart disease.

We now know that not all foods were created equal in terms of their benefits on heart health. Wholesome, natural foods such as fruits, vegetables, nuts, coconut oil, seeds, spices and fish play a key role in the prevention of heart disease. Foods like refined sugar, trans fats obtained from the processing of animal or vegetable fats, table salt and nutritionally dead white grain products are now thought to be among the worst culprits when it comes to increasing the risk of heart disease.

In fact, new research has exposed a shocking cause to heart disease and stroke. It's not cholesterol, and it's certainly not saturated fat. Just as the conventional theories on the causes of heart disease get shattered, a new one emerges: chronic inflammation. Inflammation is a powerful natural response aimed to defend the body against infection and speed up the healing of tissues. When acute inflammation is triggered, it is generally beneficial; it fights off harmful microorganisms and increases blood flow to an injured area in order to supply extra "materials" to rebuild tissues and control the loss of blood.

Problems arise when the body is constantly in a state of low-level inflammation. Chronic inflammation is unnatural and is now thought to be the root cause of modern pathologies such as diabetes, cancer, Alzheimer's disease and – yes – heart disease. Chronic inflammation alters cell metabolism, which can no longer function properly. This results in slow, degenerative tissue damage. Artery walls are no strangers to this process of slow destruction; indeed, they harden in response to inflammation and their insides become rough and chapped, increasing the likeliness of trapping circulating fat and cholesterol molecules. This is the infamous plaque build-up doctors have warned us about for years.

However, protecting your heart and arteries against inflammation is not only possible, it's also delicious! Natural foods contain healthy fats, powerful antioxidants and other phytochemicals that play a key role against chronic low-level inflammation. Antioxidants have anti-inflammatory properties that reduce the destruction of cells and preserve their ability to repair themselves.

Some particularly heart-friendly foods include spices such as turmeric, ginger and cinnamon; fish such as salmon, sardines and tuna; bright green veggies like kale and spinach; berries and melon; nuts such as cashews, almonds and walnuts; tomatoes, avocado, and even treats such as red wine, dark chocolate and tea! Consuming whole and natural foods on a daily basis is the key to fight inflammation and heart disease. Avoid sugar, as it ranks among the top culprits when it comes to inflammation.

Fortunately, this is great news. A heart-healthy cookbook no longer has to include ultra-low-fat and tasteless recipes. Instead, this cookbook contains recipes that feature some of the world's healthiest foods. Eating a balanced diet of whole and natural foods, including traditionally frowned-upon foods like eggs and coconut oil, along with moderate levels of exercise each day will help you take care of your heart. Practice yoga or meditation, as high stress levels also promote inflammation. Avoid sugar, processed foods, tobacco and get some good sleep every night. You will be amazed at how much healthier you feel!

Foods to Avoid

You will usually want to avoid:

- Refined sugar: one of the biggest sources of inflammation in our modern diet. Avoid white sugar, high-fructose corn syrup and other processed sweeteners in favour of more natural options such as raw honey and maple syrup. Make sure you consume these in small doses, since they are still concentrated sources of sugar.

- Artificial sweeteners: these unnatural substances are man-made in a lab. Our bodies see them as harmful and triggers inflammation in response. Avoid aspartame, sucralose, acesulfame-potassium, sugar alcohols and other artificial sweeteners. If you need a no-calorie sweetener, try stevia.

- Trans fats: these are by-products of the processing of natural fats. They are probably the only class of fats to limit or even avoid entirely. Instead, use some extra virgin olive oil or some coconut oil when cooking and avoid deep-fried foods, which are especially high in trans fats.

- Refined flour and grains: these have the same effect as sugar. Have small portions of wholesome quinoa or brown rice. Make your baked goods with coconut or almond flour for an extra dose of heart-healthy nutrients.

- Processed foods: high in salt, sugar or trans fats, store-bought baked goods and prepared meals don't have much to offer in terms of nutrition. Make your own meals and snacks at home. It's easy and fun, and you know exactly what you're eating.

Heart Healthy Snacks

Zucchini Fries

Prep Time: 15 minutes

Cook Time: 15 minutes

Servings: 2

INGREDIENTS

1 medium zucchini

1 cage-free egg

1/2 cup almond meal

1 teaspoon flax meal (or ground chia seed)

1/2 teaspoon paprika

1 teaspoon ground black pepper

1 teaspoon Celtic sea salt

Coconut oil (for cooking)

INSTRUCTIONS

1. Cut zucchini in half, then slice into 1/3 inch strips. Sprinkle with 1/2 teaspoon salt and place between paper towels to drain excess water. Set aside 10 minutes.
2. Heat large pan over medium-high heat and coat with coconut oil.
3. In a shallow dish, blend almond meal, flax or chia meal, and remaining spices and salt. Beat egg in small mixing bowl.
4. Gently press paper towel to absorb excess moisture from zucchini.

5. In batches, toss zucchini strips in beaten egg to lightly coat, then dredge in seasoned almond meal.

6. Carefully place coated zucchini strips into hot oil and fry about 2 minutes per side, until golden brown and heated through. Turn with tongs half way through cooking.

7. Remove from pan and drain fried on paper towel. Transfer to serving dish.

8. Serve hot with your favorite sauce.

Dill Stuffed Mushrooms

Prep Time: 15 minutes

Cook Time: 20 minutes

Servings: 2

INGREDIENTS

12 medium button mushroom caps (stems removed)

Celtic sea salt, to tastes

Ground black pepper, to taste

Dill Cream Cheese

1 cup cashews

2 sprigs fresh dill (about 1 tablespoon minced)

1 tablespoon coconut oil

1 tablespoon lemon juice

1 garlic clove

1/4 teaspoon ground white pepper (or black pepper)

1/2 teaspoon Celtic sea salt

INSTRUCTIONS

1. Preheat oven to 350 degrees F. Line sheet pan with parchment paper or baking mat.

2. Remove stems from mushroom caps, then sprinkle on salt and pepper, to taste. Place well side up on prepared sheet pan.

3. Bake 15 - 20 minutes, until golden brown and cooked through. Remove from oven and drain any liquid that has accumulated in mushroom wells. Set aside in refrigerator at least 10 minutes.

4. Peel garlic and add to food processor or high-speed blender with dill, oil, lemon juice, salt and pepper. Process until smooth, up to 5 minutes. If necessary, let mixture sit for a few minutes, then continue to process to reach desired consistency.

5. Fill cooled mushroom wells with *Dill Cream Cheese*.

6. Transfer to serving dish and serve chilled or room temperature.

Prosciutto Wrapped Dates

Prep Time: 10 minutes

Cook Time: 15 minutes

Servings: 2

INGREDIENTS

12 dried pitted dates

4 slices nitrate-free prosciutto

2/3 cup unsalted cashew butter

12 wooden toothpicks

Water

INSTRUCTIONS

1. Soak toothpicks in water about 5 minutes.
2. Preheat oven to 375 degrees F. Line sheet pan with parchment or baking mat.
3. Slice dates lengthwise and pry open. Do not separate completely. Stuff opened dates with cashew butter and re-close.
4. Cut prosciutto into thirds lengthwise. Wrap prosciutto around dates and secure with soaked toothpicks.
5. Place secured dates on prepared sheet pan. Bake for about 15 minutes, or until prosciutto is crisp and dates are heated through. Remove and let cool about 2 minutes.
6. Transfer to serving dish and serve warm. Or let cool completely and serve room temperature.

Oven-Fried Green Tomatoes

Prep Time: 5 minutes

Cook Time: 20 minutes

Servings: 4

INGREDIENTS

2 large green tomatoes

1 cup course almond meal (or pecan meal)

2 cage-free eggs

1/4 cup nut milk

1 tablespoon tapioca flour

1 tablespoon ground chia seed (or flax meal)

2 teaspoons ground black pepper

2 teaspoons Celtic sea salt

1 teaspoon smoked paprika (optional)

1/4 teaspoon dried thyme (optional)

1/4 teaspoon dried oregano (optional)

Pinch cayenne Pepper (optional)

Coconut oil (for cooking)

Spray bottle

INSTRUCTIONS

1. Preheat oven to 400 degrees F. Place wire rack in sheet pan. Add coconut oil to spray bottle and spray wire rack heavily with oil.

2. Slice tomatoes into 1/2 inch thick slices. Discard ends. Sprinkle tomatoes with 1 teaspoon salt and pepper.

3. In shallow dish, blend tapioca or arrowroot and chia or flax meal. In medium mixing bowl, blend almond or pecan meal, and remaining salt and spices. Whisk eggs, tapioca, chia and nut milk in small mixing bowl.

4. Dip tomatoes in egg mixture in batches, turning several time to coat well. Dredge in seasoned meal mixture, pressing to coat well.

5. Place coated slices on prepared sheet pan in single layer. Spray well with oil.

6. Bake for 15 - 20 minutes, until crust is golden brown and crisp and tomatoes are heated through.

7. Remove from oven and transfer to serving dish.

8. Serve hot.

Orange Anzac Biscuits

Prep Time: 5 minutes

Cook Time: 25 minutes

Servings: 12

INGREDIENTS

3/4 cup almond flour

3/4 cup sliced almonds

3/4 cup flaked or shredded coconut

1/4 cup date butter (raw honey or agave)

1/4 cup coconut oil (or ghee or cacao butter, melted)

1 orange (or tangerine or Clementine)

1/2 teaspoon baking soda

1/4 teaspoon ground ginger

INSTRUCTIONS

1. Preheat oven to 300 degrees F. Line sheet pan with parchment sheet or baking mat.

2. In medium mixing bowl, combine almond flour, sliced almonds and coconut.

3. Zest *then* juice orange into small mixings bowl. Add date butter and oil or melted butter. Mix to combine.

4. Add wet mixture to dry mixture and mix until dough comes together.

5. Form 12 large biscuits with tablespoon or scoop. Place on prepared sheet pan and flatten slightly.

6. Bake for 25 - 30 minutes, until golden. Remove from oven and let cool slightly before serving.
7. Serve warm. Or allow to cool completely and store in airtight container.

Almond Butter Crunch Granola Bar

Prep Time: 30 minutes

Servings: 8

INGREDIENTS

1 1/2 cup raw almonds

1 cup crunchy almond butter

1/4 cup flax seed (or chia seed)

1/2 cup dried pitted dates

2/3 cup shredded or flaked coconut

1/3 cup raw pumpkin seeds

1/2 teaspoon ground cinnamon

1/2 teaspoon vanilla

1 teaspoon Celtic sea salt

INSTRUCTIONS

1. Line loaf pan with parchment paper.
2. Add flax or chia to food processor or high-speed blender and process until finely ground, about 1 - 2 minutes.
3. Add 1 cup almonds and process until thick, smooth paste forms, up to 5 minutes.
4. Add dates and process until thick, fairly smooth mixture forms about 1 - 2 minutes. Transfer to medium mixing bowl.
5. Add remaining 1/2 cup almonds, almond butter, coconut, pumpkin seeds, cinnamon, vanilla, and salt. Stir to combine with large wooden spoon.

6. Transfer mixture to parchment lined pan and firmly press into bottom with hands or spatula. Place in refrigerator for 20 minutes.

7. Remove from refrigerator and cut into bars.

8. Serve chilled. Or allow to warm to room temperature and serve.

Salt and Vinegar Kale Chips

Prep Time: 10 minutes

Dehydrating Time: 4 - 6 hours

Servings: 4

INGREDIENTS

2 kale heads (or 1.5 - 2 lbs kale leaves)

3 tablespoons coconut oil (or walnut, almond or sesame oil.)

1 tablespoon coconut aminos (or tamari or liquid aminos)

1 tablespoon coconut vinegar (or apple cider vinegar)

1 tablespoon Celtic sea salt

INSTRUCTIONS

1. Wash and spin dry kale. Remove tough spine and chop or tear into pieces.

2. Add kale pieces to large mixing bowl with oil, aminos, vinegar and salt and spices. Toss to coat.

3. Add single layer of coated kale to dehydrator tray and place in dehydrator. Dehydrate at 115 degrees F for 4 - 6 hours, depending on desired crispiness.

4. Remove kale from dehydrator and transfer to serving dish.

5. Serve immediately. Or store in airtight container.

Chocolate Chip Trail Mix

Prep Time: 5 minutes

Servings: 4

INGREDIENTS

1/2 cup raw almonds

1/2 cup raw pumpkin seeds

1/2 cup cashews

1/4 cup golden raisins

1/2 cup organic dark chocolate chips (or chocolate bark or cacao nibs)

INSTRUCTIONS

1. Roughly chop chocolate bark, if using. Add chocolate or cacao nibs to medium mixing bowl with raisins and nuts. Mix to combine.

2. Transfer to serving dish and serve immediately. Or store in cool dry place in airtight container.

Tart Cherry Energy Bar

Prep Time: 25 minutes

Servings: 6

INGREDIENTS

1 cup dried tart cherries

1/4 cup dried pitted dates

1/3 cup warm water

1 lime

1 cup raw almonds

1/4 teaspoon ground ginger

1/4 teaspoon vanilla

1/8 teaspoon Celtic sea salt

INSTRUCTIONS

1. Zest and juice lime into small mixing bowl. Add warm water and dried cherries. Toss to coat and set aside 10 minutes.

2. Line loaf pan with parchment paper.

3. Add nuts and dates to food processor or high-speed blender. Drain soaked cherries and add to processor with cinnamon, vanilla and salt. Process for about 1 minute, until mixture is coarsely ground and sticks together when pressed.

4. Scrape mixture into prepared loaf pan and press firmly into bottom with hands or spatula.

5. Place in refrigerator and chill for 10 minutes. Remove and cut into 6 bars.

6. Serve immediately. Or store in refrigerator up to 2 weeks.

Simple Almond Apricot Balls

Prep Time: 15 minutes

Servings: 12

INGREDIENTS

1/2 cup dried pitted dates

1/3 cup dried apricots

1/3 cup almonds (toasted or roasted, if preferred)

1/4 cup flaked or shredded coconut

1/2 tablespoon raw honey (or agave)

INSTRUCTIONS

1. Add apricots and dates to food processor or high-speed blender. Process until finely chopped, about 1 - 2 minutes.

2. Add almonds and coconut to processor. Process until well ground, about 2 minutes. Add honey and pulse until mixture sticks together, about 30 seconds.

3. Form mixture into 12 balls.

4. Serve immediately. Or store in airtight container in refrigerator up to 2 weeks.

Sweet Potato Evening Bites

Prep time: 10 minutes

Cook time: 30 minutes

INGREDIENTS

3 sweet potatoes

¼ cup extra virgin olive oil

¼ tsp Celtic sea salt

¼ tsp smoked paprika

INSTRUCTIONS

1. Preheat oven to 500 degrees.
2. Peel the potatoes and cut them into small wedges. In a large bowl, combine potato wedges, extra virgin olive oil, Celtic sea salt and smoked paprika. Mix well until all wedges are coated in all ingredients.
3. Place on a baking sheet and bake for 30 minutes, turning once halfway through, and continue cooking until they are well browned.
4. Remove from oven and let cool. Serve.

Baby Carrot with Tahini

Prep time: 3 minutes

INGREDIENTS

2 tbsp organic Tahini

1 tsp cinnamon

½ cup baby carrots

1 stalk celery

INSTRUCTIONS

1. Slice the celery stalk into small pieces, about the size of the baby carrots.
2. In a very small bowl, mix the tahini and cinnamon together.
3. Serve. Eat by dipping the vegetables in the tahini/cinnamon mix.

Icy Blueberry Delight

Prep time: 5 minutes

INGREDIENTS

¼ cup coconut milk

1 cup blueberries

½ cup plums

½ cup raspberries

½ cup ice cubes

INSTRUCTIONS

1. Remove pits from plums.
2. Combine all the ingredients in a blender and blend until pureed.
3. Serve.

Homemade Choco Raisins

Prep time: 30 minutes

INGREDIENTS

1 cup raisins

two 1.4 oz bars of Enjoy Life Boom Choco Boom Dark Chocolate

INSTRUCTIONS

1. Boil water in a large saucepan. Cover the saucepan with a mesh top and place a small saucepan on top. Place the chocolate bars in the small saucepan and use the steam to melt them.

2. In a bowl, combine melted chocolate and raisins.

3. Place raisins on a wax paper sheet and place them in the freezer for 15 minutes to harden.

4. Serve.

Strawberry Creamy Blast

Prep time: 3 minutes

INGREDIENTS

3 oz tuna

½ avocado

¼ tsp ground black pepper

½ cup blueberries

½ cup strawberries

INSTRUCTIONS

1. Mix tuna and avocado into a paste. Add ground black pepper and combine.
2. Chop strawberries and add them into blueberries.
3. Place both tuna and fruit mixtures on a plate and serve.

Spicy Chicken Wraps

Prep time: 5 minutes

Cook time: 3 minutes

INGREDIENTS

4 slices of chicken deli meat

1 tbsp olive oil

1 small onion

1 red bell pepper

1 avocado

¼ tsp garlic powder

INSTRUCTIONS

1. Remove the nut from the avocado and mash it into a paste. Chop the pepper and onion into small pieces.
2. Combine the garlic powder, pepper and onion in the bowl with the avocado and mix well.
3. Add the olive oil in a pan over low heat and heat the chicken mildly, turning frequently, for 3 minutes.
4. Remove the chicken from heat and place ¼ of the avocado/pepper/onion mixture onto each piece.
5. Wrap the chicken up into tubes and serve.

Ants On A Log

Prep Time: 5 minutes

Cook Time: 5 minutes

Servings: 2

INGREDIENTS

3 celery stalks

2 tablespoons raisins

Cashew Butter

1 cup cashews

1 teaspoon coconut oil

1/2 teaspoon ground cinnamon

INSTRUCTIONS

1. Add cashews, cinnamon, and coconut oil to food processor or bullet blender. Process until smooth. Let mixture rest between periods of processing to reach desired consistency, if necessary.
2. Cut celery stakes into thirds and fill wells with *Cashew Butter*. Place raisins on cashew butter.
3. Serve room temperature. Or refrigerate 10 minutes and serve chilled.

Grilled Pineapple Fruit Salad

Prep Time: 5 minutes

Cook Time: 10 minutes

Servings: 4

INGREDIENTS

1/2 pineapple

1 peach

1 cup fresh cherries

1 orange

1 tablespoon fresh mint leaves

Half lemon

INSTRUCTIONS

1. Heat griddle or grill over medium-high heat. Lightly coat with coconut oil.

2. Peel and core pineapple. Cut into half inch slices. Place slice on griddle and grill about 4 - 5 minutes on each side, until grill marks appear and sugars caramelized.

3. Cut peach in half and grill flesh side down for about 5 minutes.

4. Pit cherries and slice in half. Peel orange and cut flesh from white cellulose film and pith.

5. Chop pineapple and peach. Add to medium mixing bowl with cherries and orange wedges. Chiffon mint. Add to bowl and squeeze on lemon juice. Toss to combine.

6. Serve room temperature. Or refrigerate and serve chilled.

Fruit 'N Nut Bars

Prep Time: 10 minutes

Cook Time: 10 minutes

Servings: 6

INGREDIENTS

1/4 cup dried cherries

1/2 cup dried apricots

1/4 cup dried cranberries

1/4 cup dried dates

1/3 cup warm water

1 cup cashews

1/2 teaspoon vanilla

1/2 teaspoon ground cinnamon

1/4 teaspoon ground ginger

1/4 teaspoon sea salt

INSTRUCTIONS

1. Soak dried fruit in warm water for 5 - 10 minutes. Drain and add to food processor or bullet blender with cashews, vanilla, cinnamon, ginger and salt.

2. Process until mixture forms a sticky mass, about 1 minute.

3. Transfer to loaf pan lined with parchment. Fold parchment over mixture and press firmly into bottom of pan with spatula or hand.

4. Refrigerate for 10 minutes. Remove and cut into 6 bars.

5. Serve chilled or room temperature.

Simple Guacamole

Prep Time: 5 minutes

Cook Time: 5 minutes

Servings: 4

INGREDIENTS

2 avocados

1 shallot

1 small tomato

1 bunch cilantro

Half lime

2 teaspoons paprika

1/2 teaspoon ground cumin

1/2 teaspoon ground black pepper

1/2 teaspoon sea salt

INSTRUCTIONS

1. Peel and finely dice shallot. Dice tomato and cilantro. Add to small mixing bowl.
2. Slice avocados in half, pit, and scoop flesh into bowl. Add 1 teaspoon paprika, 1/2 teaspoon cumin, 1/2 teaspoon black pepper and 1/2 teaspoon salt.
3. Mash avocado and mix ingredients well with fork. Transfer to serving dish and squeeze on juice of half a lime. Sprinkle with remaining teaspoon of paprika.
4. Serve immediately. Or refrigerate 30 minutes, and serve chilled.

Coconut Shrimp

Prep Time: 10 minutes

Cook Time: 15 minutes

Servings: 4

INGREDIENTS

3 egg whites

1 lb large shrimp

1 cup flaked coconut

1/2 teaspoon garlic powder

1/2 teaspoon ground white pepper (or ground black pepper)

1 teaspoon sea salt

Coconut oil (for cooking)

Mango Salsa

1 ripe mango

1/2 small white onion

1 small jalapeño

Juice of half lime

INSTRUCTIONS

1. Preheat oven to 425 degrees F. Line sheet pan with parchment paper. Or place oven-safe wire rack over sheet pan.
2. Add coconut to shallow dish.
3. Beat egg whites with salt, pepper and garlic powder in a large mixing bowl with hand mixer or whisk until light and fluffy.

4. Peel and devein shrimp. Leave tails on. Add shrimp to egg whites to coat.

5. Let excess egg white drain from shrimp, then add to coconut flakes. Toss to coat. Return shrimp to egg whites, then coconut flakes again. Press shrimp into coconut and coat well.

6. Place the shrimp on prepared sheet pan. Brush lightly with liquid coconut oil.

7. Place in oven and bake for 5 - 7 minutes. Then turn shrimp over, brush with coconut oil, and bake another 5 - 7 minutes, until coconut is golden brown and shrimp are bright pink.

8. For *Mango Salsa*, slice mango around pit. Peel and dice flesh. Peel and dice onion. Mince jalapeño, discarding seeds and stem. Add to small serving dish juice of half a lime. Mix to combine.

9. Remove shrimp from oven and allow to cool for a few minutes.

10. Serve warm with *Mango Salsa*.

Avocado Cashew Hummus with Cucumber

Prep Time: 5 minutes*

Servings: 4

INGREDIENTS

1 cup raw cashews

1 avocado

Juice of 1/2 lemon

2 garlic cloves

1 teaspoon ground white pepper (or 1/2 teaspoon ground black pepper)

Small bunch fresh cilantro

1/2 teaspoon Celtic sea salt

1 small cucumber

Water

INSTRUCTIONS

1. *Soak cashews in enough water to cover at least 4 hours, or overnight in refrigerator. Drain and rinse.

2. Peel garlic. Juice lemon. Remove cilantro leaves from stem. Add to food processor or high-speed blender with soaked cashews, salt and pepper.

3. Slice avocado in half. Remove pit and scoop flesh into processor. Process until smooth, about 1 - 2 minutes. Add water or raw oil to reach desired consistency, if necessary.

4. Transfer mixture to serving dish.

5. Peel cucumber if desired. Cut diagonally into 1/3 inch slices. Arrange on serving dish.

6. Serve immediately with hummus. Or place in refrigerator for 20 minutes, then serve chilled.

Cocoa Date Spread

Prep Time: 5 minutes*

Servings: 4

INGREDIENTS

10 - 12 oz dried pitted dates

2 cups water

3 tablespoons raw cocoa powder

1/2 teaspoon ground cinnamon

1/4 teaspoon ground ginger

Ground black pepper, to taste

INSTRUCTIONS

1. *Soak dates in water overnight. Drain and reserve 1/4 cup liquid.

2. Add soaked dates, cocoa powder, cinnamon, ginger and black pepper to taste to food processor or high-speed blender. Pulse until chunky mixture forms. Add reserved liquid to reach desired consistency, if necessary.

3. Or add dates to medium mixing bowl with cocoa powder, cinnamon, ginger and black pepper to taste. Mash with large fork or potato masher for about 5 minutes, until chunky mixture forms. Add reserved liquid to reach desired consistency, if necessary.

4. Transfer to serving dish and serve with fruits, veggies, or raw crackers and breads.

Cashew Spinach Dip with Bell Pepper

Prep Time: 10 minutes

Servings: 2

INGREDIENTS

2 - 3 cups spinach leaves

1 1/2 cups raw cashews

3 garlic cloves

1 lemon

1/3 cup water

1/4 teaspoon mustard powder (or mustard seeds)

1/2 teaspoon ground white pepper (or 1/4 teaspoon ground black pepper)

1/2 teaspoon Celtic sea salt

1 red bell pepper

INSTRUCTIONS

1. Cut bell pepper in half and remove seeds, veins and stems. Slice peppers into 1 - 1 1/2 inch strips. Arrange on serving dish and set aside.

2. Juice lemon. Peel garlic. Add to food processor or high-speed blender with cashews and mustard powder or seeds. Process until finely ground, about 2 minutes.

3. Add salt, pepper and water. Process until smooth. Add spinach and pulse until spinach is desired texture.

4. Transfer mixture to serving dish. Serving immediately with bell pepper slices. Or refrigerate 20 minutes and serve chilled.

Sweet Carrot Raisin Salad

Prep Time: 5 minutes

Servings: 2

INSTRUCTIONS

2 large carrots

2 tablespoons red raisins

2 tablespoons golden raisins

1/4 cup raw slivered almonds (or sliced almonds)

1/2 small orange (or tangerine)

1/4 teaspoon ground cinnamon

DIRECTIONS

1. Add carrots to food processor with shredding attachment and process, or grate with grater. Add to medium mixing bowl with raisins, almonds and cinnamon.
2. Zest *then* juice orange. Add to carrot mixture and toss to combine.
3. Transfer to serving dishes and serve immediately. Or refrigerate 20 minutes and serve chilled.

Fresh Zesty Pico de Gallo

Prep Time: 15 minutes*

Servings: 4

INGREDIENTS

4 plum tomatoes

1/2 small red onion

Small bunch fresh cilantro

1/2 jalapeño pepper

1/2 lime

1 garlic clove

1/8 teaspoon garlic powder

1/4 teaspoon ground cumin

1/4 teaspoon Celtic sea salt

1/4 teaspoon ground black pepper

INSTRUCTIONS

1. Finely dice tomatoes. Peel and dice onion. Add to medium mixing bowl.
2. Finely chop cilantro. Remove seeds, veins and stem from jalapeño, then mince. Peel and mince garlic. Add to tomatoes with salt, spices and squeeze of lime. Mix until well combined.
3. Transfer mixture to serving dish
4. *Refrigerate 3 hours. Serve room temperature or chilled with raw chips.

Sardine & Avocado on Endives

Prep Time: 5 minutes

Cook Time:

Servings: 4

INGREDIENTS

1-2 bunches endives

1 tin sardines in olive oil

1 Tablespoon apple cider vinegar

1 Tablespoon lemon juice

2 Tablespoons fresh parsley

1 avocado, halved, pitted, and chopped

½ teaspoon sea salt

INSTRUCTIONS

1. In a medium bowl, combine the sardines, vinegar, parsley, and lemon juice. Marinate the sardines for about 30 minutes in the refrigerator.
2. In the meantime, remove the leaves from the endives, wash them, and pat them dry. Set them on a platter, with the "cup" side facing up.
3. After the sardines are chilled, mix in the avocados. Use a spoon to divide the mixture among the endive leaves. There should be enough mixture to fill about 12 leaves.

Smoked Salmon Bites

Prep Time: 10 minutes

Cook Time: N/A

Servings: 2

INGREDIENTS

1 large seedless cucumber

4 oz smoked salmon

1 avocado

½ red onion

1 Tablespoon lemon juice

1/2 teaspoon sea salt

Chives for garnish (optional)

INSTRUCTIONS

1. Slice the cucumber into ¾-inch thick slices.
2. Slice the smoked salmon into 1-inch by 1-inch pieces.
3. In a small bowl, mash the avocado with the salt, lemon juice, and onion.
4. Spread the avocado mash evenly across each of the cucumber slices.
5. Top each cucumber with a piece of the smoked salmon.
6. Garnish with a chive, if desired.

Ginger Spice Cookies

Prep Time: 15 minutes

Cook Time: 15 minutes

Servings: 6

INGREDIENTS

1 1/2 cups almond flour

1 cage-free egg

1/4 cup sweetener*

2 tablespoons coconut oil

1 teaspoon ground chia seed (or flax meal)

1/4 teaspoon baking soda

1 tablespoon ground ginger

1/2 teaspoon ground clove

Pinch all spice

Pinch ground black pepper

Pinch sea salt

INSTRUCTIONS

1. Preheat oven to 350 degrees F. Line sheet pan with parchment or baking mat, or lightly coat with coconut oil.
2. Beat egg, oil, sweetener and chia meal in medium mixing bowl with hand mixer or whisk.
3. Add almond flour, baking soda, salt and spices. Mix until combined.
4. Chill batter in freezer for 5 - 10 minutes.

5. Scoop chilled batter into 6 large rounds on prepared sheet pan. Press into disk shape with hand.
6. Bake for about 15 minutes, until firm around the edges and golden brown.
7. Remove from oven and let cool about 10 minutes.
8. Serve warm. Or let cool completely and serve room temperature.

raw honey, agave nectar, grade B maple syrup, molasses

Orange Cranberry Muffins

Prep Time: 5 minutes

Cook Time: 20 minutes

Servings: 12

INGREDIENTS

1 1/2 cups almond flour

2 cage-free eggs

1/2 cup fresh squeezed orange juice (about 2 oranges)

1/4 cup coconut oil

1/4 cup dried cranberries

1 tablespoon orange zest

1 teaspoon baking powder

1/2 teaspoon vanilla

1/2 teaspoon sea salt

INSTRUCTIONS

1. Preheat oven to 350 degrees F. Line muffin pan with paper liners or coconut oil.
2. In medium bowl, beat eggs with hand mixer or whisk until light and a foamy. Add coconut oil, orange juice and zest. Beat well.
3. Sift in almond flour, baking powder, vanilla and salt. Mix until combined. Stir in cranberries.
4. Use ice cream scoop or tablespoon to scoop batter into prepared muffin pan.

5. Bake about 20 minutes, or until toothpick inserted into center comes out clean.
6. Remove from oven and serve warm. Or let cool completely and serve room temperature.

NOTE: Bake in oiled loaf pan for 40 - 45 minutes for **Cranberry Orange Bread**.

stevia, raw honey or agave nectar

Spinach Mushroom Muffins

Prep Time: 10 minutes

Cook Time: 15 minutes

Servings: 12

INGREDIENTS

1 cup almond flour

2 eggs

1 cup fresh spinach

1/2 cup fresh mushrooms

1 tablespoon sweetener*

1 tablespoon apple cider vinegar

1 teaspoon baking soda

1 teaspoon baking powder

1 teaspoon ground white pepper (or black pepper)

1/2 teaspoon ground nutmeg

1/2 teaspoon dried basil

INSTRUCTIONS

1. Preheat oven to 350 degrees F. Line muffin pan with paper liners or lightly coat with coconut oil. Heat medium pan over medium-high heat.

2. Slice mushrooms and add to hot pan. Sauté about 3 minutes, then add spinach. Sauté until water evaporates, mushrooms are cooked through and spinach is wilted. Set aside.

3. Beat eggs, sweetener and vinegar in medium mixing bowl with hand mixer or whisk until thick and frothy.

4. Add sautéed veggies, almond flour, baking soda and powder and spices and mix until combined.

5. Use ice cream scoop or tablespoon to pour batter into prepared muffin pan.

6. Bake 15 - 20 minutes, until edges are golden brown and tops are firm.

7. Remove muffins from oven and let cool about 5 minutes.

8. Serve warm. Or allow to cool complete and serve temperature.

NOTE: Bake in square oiled baking pan for 30 - 35 minutes for **Spinach Mushroom Bread**.

stevia, raw honey or agave nectar

Health Conscious Baking

Citrus Herb Anzac Biscuits

Prep Time: 5 minutes

Cook Time: 25 minutes

Servings: 4

INGREDIENTS

3/4 cup almond flour

3/4 cup sliced almonds

3/4 cup flaked or shredded coconut

1/4 cup raw honey (or agave, date butter, or stevia)

1/4 cup coconut oil

1/2 lemon

1/2 orange (or tangerine or Clementine)

1 sprig fresh rosemary

1/2 teaspoon baking soda

1 tablespoon water

INSTRUCTIONS

1. Preheat oven to 300 degrees F. Line sheet pan with parchment sheet or baking mat.
2. In medium mixing bowl, combine almond flour, sliced almonds and coconut.
3. Mix baking soda and water in small mixing bowl. Add to medium mixing bowl with sweetener and oil.

4. Zest *then* juice citrus into mixing bowl. Remove rosemary needles from stem and mince. Add to bowl. Mix until combined. Add water 1 tablespoon at a time if dough is too crumbly.

5. Form 12 large biscuits and arrange on sheet pan. Flatten slightly with hand for even baking. Bake for 25 - 30 minutes, until golden.

6. Remove from oven and transfer to wire rack to cool completely. Once cooled, place in airtight container and store in freezer. Place small parchment sheets in between servings, if desired.

7. To serve, remove from freezer and let thaw about 1 hour. Or place in WARM oven until warmed through.

Pure Pumpkin Bread

Prep Time: 5 minutes

Cook Time: 40 minutes

Servings: 8

INGREDIENTS

1 cup almond flour

3/4 cup coconut flour

15 oz (1 can) pumpkin puree

2 cage-free eggs

1/2 cup nut milk

1/2 cup unsweetened applesauce

1/4 cup coconut oil (or coconut or cacao butter, melted) (or nut butter)

1/4 cup raw honey (or agave, date butter or stevia)

1/4 cup pumpkin seeds

2 teaspoons baking soda

1 tablespoon ground cinnamon

1 teaspoon ground nutmeg

1 teaspoon Celtic sea salt

1/2 teaspoon ground black pepper (optional)

Coconut oil (for cooking)

INSTRUCTIONS

1. Preheat oven to 350 degrees F. Coat medium loaf pan with coconut oil.

2. Add eggs, oil or butter, applesauce, nut milk and sweetener to food processor or high-speed blender. Process until thick and light, about 1 - 2 minutes.

3. Add pumpkin, salt and spices. Process to incorporate.

4. Add flour and baking soda to small mixing bowl and stir to combine. Add to processor in batches and process until well combined.

5. Pour batter into prepared loaf pan and bake 35 - 40 minutes, until firm but springy in the center.

6. Remove from oven and set aside to cool.

7. Slice and serve warm. Or allow to cool completely and serve room temperature.

Nutty Apple Crumble

Prep Time: 20 minutes

Cook Time: 50 minutes

Servings: 8

INGREDIENTS

Crust

2 cups almond flour

1 cage-free egg

2 tablespoons coconut oil (or cacao butter or ghee)

1/4 teaspoon Celtic sea salt

Filling

5 apples

1/2 cup date butter (or raw honey or agave)

1/2 lemon

1 teaspoon ground cinnamon

1/2 teaspoon vanilla

1/4 teaspoon ground nutmeg

1/4 teaspoon Celtic sea salt

Topping

1/2 cup almond flour

1/2 cup pecans

1/2 cup shredded coconut

1/4 cup cold cacao butter (or coconut butter, ghee or coconut oil)

1/4 cup raw honey (or agave)

1/4 cup dried pitted dates

2 tablespoons ground flax

1 teaspoon cinnamon

INSTRUCTIONS

1. Preheat oven to 375 degrees F.
2. For *Crust*, blend almond flour and salt in small mixing bowl. Add egg and oil or butter. Mix until dough forms. Press into pie pan or baking dish with hand or wooden spoon. Set aside.
3. For *Filling*, core and peel apples. Cut into thin slices and add to large mixing bowl. Add sweetener, salt and spices. Juice 1/2 lemon over apples and mix to combine. Press apples firmly into *Crust*.
4. For *Topping*, add dates and honey or agave to food processor or high-speed blender. Process until coarsely ground, about 1 minute. Add butter or oil, almond flour, pecans, coconut, flax and cinnamon. Pulse until finely chopped or coarsely ground. Sprinkle *Topping* over apples.
5. Bake 40 - 50 minutes, until apples are cooked and *Topping* is browned and crisp.
6. Remove from oven and allow to cool at least 5 minutes.
7. Slice and serve warm. Or let cool completed and serve room temperature.

Gingerbread Cookies

Prep Time: 5 minutes

Cook Time: 15 minutes

Servings: 12

INGREDIENTS

1 cup almond flour

2 cage-free eggs

1/2 cup dried pitted dates

1/4 cup raw honey (or dark agave)

1/4 cup coconut oil (or cacao butter, melted)

1/2 teaspoon baking soda

1/2 teaspoon baking powder

2 teaspoons ground ginger

1 teaspoon ground cinnamon

1 teaspoon vanilla

1/2 teaspoon ground cloves

1/2 teaspoon ground black pepper

1/4 teaspoon Celtic sea salt

Natural sarsaparilla or root beer beverage, or nut milk (optional)

INSTRUCTIONS

1. Preheat oven to 350 degrees F. Line sheet pan with parchment or
    baking mat.

2. Add dates, honey or agave and eggs to food processor or high-speed blender. Process until thick smooth mixture forms, about 2 minutes.

3. Add almond flour, oil or butter, baking soda and powder, salt and spices to processor. Process until thick mixture comes together, about 1 minute. Add sarsaparilla, root beer or nut milk to thin as necessary. Batter should resemble thick cookie dough.

4. From rounds and place on prepares sheet pan. Flatten into disks.

5. Bake 10 - 15 minutes, until browned around edges and cooked through, but still soft.

6. Remove from oven and let cool at about 10 minutes.

7. Transfer to serving dish and serve warm. Or cool completely and serve room temperature.

Strawberry Toaster Pastry

Prep Time: 25 minutes

Cook Time: 20 minutes

Servings: 4

INSTRUCTIONS

Crust

2 cups almond flour

2 cage-free eggs

1/4 cup coconut oil (or ghee, cacao butter or coconut butter, softened)

1 tablespoon date butter (or honey or agave)

1/4 teaspoon baking soda

1/4 teaspoon vanilla

1/2 teaspoon Celtic sea salt

Filling

2 cups chopped strawberries (about 3/4 pint whole strawberries) (fresh or frozen)

2 tablespoons raw honey (or agave)

1/2 teaspoon vanilla

1/4 teaspoon Celtic sea salt

INSTRUCTIONS

1. Preheat oven to 400 degrees. Line sheet pan with parchment or baking mat. Cover cutting board with parchment.

2. For *Crust*, sift almond flour into medium mixing bowl. Add baking soda, vanilla and salt.

3. In a small mixing bowl, whisk eggs and date butter. Add flour mixture and mix to combine. Add oil, ghee or butter and mix until malleable dough comes together.

4. Roll in plastic wrap or wrap tightly in parchment and refrigerate for 15 minutes.

5. Heat medium pan over medium heat.

6. Chop strawberries and add to hot pan with honey, vanilla and salt. Cook strawberries down until juices thicken and reduce, about 10 minutes. Stir occasionally.

7. Remove dough from refrigerator. Roll out dough on parchment covered cutting board to about 1/8 inch thick rectangle with rolling pin. Use sharp knife or pizza cutter to cut dough into 4 rectangles.

8. Scoop equal portions of *Filling* into center of one side of each dough rectangle. Fold bare half of dough over filled half. Press edges together, letting any trapped air escape. Crimp edges of dough together with fork. Repeat with remaining dough.

9. Arrange pastries on prepared sheet pan and bake 15 - 20 minutes, or until golden and cooked through.

10. Remove from oven and serve immediately. Or allow to cool and serve room temperature.

11. Reheat in toaster, if preferred.

Cocoa Zucchini Muffin

Prep Time: 10 minutes

Cook Time: 15 minutes

Servings: 12

INGREDIENTS

1 1/2 cups almond flour

2 cage-free eggs

1 small zucchini (about 1 cup grated)

1/2 cup unsweetened applesauce

1/4 cup date butter (or agave or raw honey)

1/4 cup coconut oil (or cacao or coconut butter, melted)

1/4 cup cocoa powder

2 tablespoons ground chia seed (or flax meal)

1 teaspoon baking soda

1 teaspoon baking powder

1 teaspoon vanilla

1 teaspoon ground cinnamon

1 teaspoon ground black pepper

1/2 teaspoon Celtic sea salt

1/4 cup cocoa nibs or chocolate chips (optional)

INSTRUCTIONS

1. Preheat oven to 350 degrees F. Line muffin pan with paper liners or lightly coat with coconut oil.

2. Add eggs, oil or melted butter, applesauce and date butter to food processor or high-speed blender. Process until thick, light mixture forms, about 1 - 2 minutes.

3. Sift almond flour, cocoa powder, chia or flax meal, baking soda and powder, salt and spices into processor. Process to combine, about 1 minute.

4. Grate zucchini and stir in with cocoa nibs or chocolate chips (optional).

5. Use scoop or tablespoon to pour batter into prepared muffin pan. Bake for about 15 - 20 minutes, until toothpick inserted into center comes out clean.

6. Remove from oven and let cool about 5 minutes.

7. Serve warm. Or let cool completely and serve room temperature.

Sweet Cherry Fig Newtons

Prep Time: 10 minutes

Cook Time: 15 minutes

Servings: 12

INSTRUCTIONS

Cookie Dough

1 1/2 cups almond flour

1/4 cup dried pitted dates

1/4 cup date butter (or agave or honey)

1/4 cup coconut oil (or cacao or coconut butter, melted)

1 teaspoon vanilla

1/4 teaspoon Celtic sea salt

Cherry Fig Filling

1/2 cup dried black mission figs

1/4 cup pitted cherries (fresh or thawed)

1/4 teaspoon ground ginger

INSTRUCTIONS

1. Preheat oven to 350 degrees F. Line sheet pan with parchment or baking mat.
2. For *Cookie Dough*, Add dried dates, date butter, and oil or melted butter to food processor or high-speed blender. Process until coarsely ground, about 1 - 2 minutes.

3. Sift almond flour and salt into medium mixing bowl. Add date mixture to flour mixture and mix to combine. Set aside.

4. For *Filling*, remove stems from figs and add to clean food processor or high-speed blender with cherries and ginger. Process until smooth mixture forms, about 2 minutes. Set aside.

5. Divide dough in half. Roll first half of dough into long, thin rectangle about 1/4 inch thick between 2 parchment sheets.

6. Spread 1/2 of *Cherry Fig Filling* along one side of the dough, long-ways.

7. Use parchment to fold dough in half along long edge so plain dough covers side with *Cherry Fig Filling*. Dough should resemble flattened log.

8. Press edges of dough together for tight seal. Place on prepared sheet pan. Repeat with remaining *Cookie Dough* and *Cherry Fig Filling*.

9. Bake for 12 - 15 minutes, or until the edges are golden brown.

10. Remove from the oven and let cool about 5 minutes. Then slice logs into 2 inch cookies.

11. Serve immediately. Or allow to cool completely and serve room temperature.

Lemon Coconut Pinwheel Cookies

Prep Time: 10 minutes

Cook Time: 20 minutes

Servings: 12

INGREDIENTS

Dough

2 cups almond flour

1 cage-free egg

2 tablespoon raw honey (or agave or date butter)

1 teaspoon vanilla

1/2 teaspoon baking powder

1/4 teaspoon Celtic sea salt

Filling

1/4 cup shredded or flaked coconut

1 lemon

2 tablespoons raw honey (or agave or date butter)

INSTRUCTIONS

1. Preheat oven to 300 degrees F. Line sheet pan with parchment or baking mat. Prepare 2 additional sheets of parchment.
2. For *Dough*, add flour, egg, honey, vanilla, baking powder and salt to medium mixing bowl. Blend with wooden spoon, then knead with hands to form thick dough, about 1 minute.
3. Divide dough in half. Place half of dough in small mixing bowl.

4. For *Filling*, add zest then juice lemon into small bowl. Add honey and coconut. Mix until well combined.

5. Roll out each half of dough separately on parchment sheets. Roll into equal rectangles.

6. Place *Filling* rectangle on top of plain dough. Use parchment to help roll dough tightly along long edge into log.

7. Use sharp knife to cut log into 1/4 thick round slices. Place cookies on prepared sheet pan. Bake for about 10 minutes, until edges are golden brown.

8. Remove from oven and let cool about 5 minutes.

9. Serve warm. Or let cool completely and serve room temperature.

Pineapple Coconut Cake

Prep Time: 10 minutes

Cook Time: 45 minutes

Servings: 12

INGREDIENTS

6 cage-free eggs

3/4 cup coconut flour

1 cup flaked coconut

1 1/2 cups pineapple (diced)

1/2 cup raw honey (or agave or date butter)

1/2 cup coconut oil (or cacao or coconut butter, melted)

1 teaspoon baking soda

1 teaspoon baking powder

1 teaspoon vanilla

1/2 teaspoon Celtic sea salt

INSTRUCTIONS

1. Preheat oven to 350 degrees F. Lightly coat square or rectangular baking dish with coconut oil.
2. Add eggs to food processor or high-speed blender. Process until pale and lightened, about 2 minutes.
3. Add flour, coconut, pineapple, sweetener, oil or butter, baking soda, baking powder, vanilla and salt. Process until well combined, about 1 - 2 minutes.

4. Pour batter into prepared baking dish and bake about 45 minutes, until golden brown and firm in the center.
5. Remove from oven and allow to cool about 10 minutes.
6. Slice and serve warm. Or let cool completely and serve room temperature.

Sweet Banana Shortbreads

Prep Time: 10 minutes

Cook Time: 30 minutes

Servings: 12

INGREDIENTS

1 cup coconut flour

2 overripe bananas

2 cage-free eggs

1/4 cup raw honey (or agave or date butter)

1/4 cup coconut oil (coconut or cacao butter)

1 teaspoon baking powder

1/2 teaspoon ground cinnamon

1/2 teaspoon vanilla

1/2 teaspoon of Celtic sea salt

INSTRUCTIONS

1. Preheat oven to 350 degrees F. Line sheet pan with baking mat or lightly coat with coconut oil.
2. Add eggs to food processor or high-speed blender and process until light and fluffy, about 2 minutes. Peel and add bananas, sweetener, oil or butter, cinnamon and vanilla. Process until well combined.
3. Add almond flour, baking powder and salt. Process until dough comes together.
4. Roll dough into 12 balls and place on prepared sheet pan. Press to flatten.

5. Bake 10 - 15 minutes, until golden around edges.

6. Remove from oven and allow to cool at least 5 minutes.

7. Serve warm. Or transfer to wire rack to cool completely and serve room temperature.

Cranberry Almond Cookies

Prep Time: 10 minutes

Cook Time: 15 minutes

Servings: 12

INGREDIENTS

1 1/2 cups almond flour

1 cage-free egg

1/4 cup coconut oil (or cacao or coconut butter)

1/4 cup raw honey (or agave or date butter)

1/4 cup almond butter

1/4 cup almonds

1/4 cup dried cranberries

1/2 teaspoon baking powder

1 teaspoon vanilla

1/4 teaspoon Celtic sea salt

INSTRUCTIONS

1. Preheat oven to 350 degrees F. Line sheet pan with parchment or baking mat.
2. Sift flour, baking powder and salt into medium mixing bowl. Beat with whisk or hand mixer to lighten. Add egg, oil or butter, sweetener, almond butter, vanilla and salt. Mix well to form dough.
3. Chop almonds and add to bowl with cranberries. Mix to combine.

4. Shape dough into 12 balls and place on prepared baking sheet. Flatten slightly with hand or spatula.

5. Place in oven and bake 10 - 15 minutes, until golden brown along edges.

6. Remove from oven and let cool 5 minutes.

7. Serve warm. Or transfer to wire rack to cool completely and serve room temperature.

Walnut Raisin Cookies

Prep Time: 10 minutes

Cook Time: 15 minutes

Servings: 12

INGREDIENTS

1 1/4 cups almond flour

1 cage-free egg

1/4 cup coconut oil (or cacao or coconut butter)

1/4 cup raw honey (or agave or date butter)

1/4 cup cashew butter

1/2 cup walnuts

1/4 cup raisins

1 teaspoon baking powder

1 teaspoon vanilla

1/4 teaspoon Celtic sea salt

INSTRUCTIONS

1. Preheat oven to 350 degrees F. Line sheet pan with parchment or baking mat.
2. Sift flour, baking powder and salt into medium mixing bowl. Beat with whisk or hand mixer to lighten. Add egg, oil or butter, sweetener, cashew butter, vanilla and salt. Mix well to form dough.
3. Chop walnuts and add to bowl with raisins. Mix to combine.

4. Shape dough into 12 balls and place onto prepared baking sheet. Flatten slightly with hand or spatula.

5. Place in oven and bake 10 - 15 minutes, until golden brown along edges.

6. Remove from oven and let cool 5 minutes.

7. Serve warm. Or transfer to wire rack to cool completely and serve room temperature.

Cinnamon Raisin Bread

Prep Time: 5 minutes

Cook Time: 20 minutes

Servings: 12

INGREDIENTS

3/4 cup coconut flour

3/4 cup almond flour

1/4 cup ground chia seed (or flax meal)

2 cage-free eggs

1/2 cup raisins

1/2 cup coconut oil

1/2 cup unsweetened applesauce

1/4 cup sweetener*

2 tablespoons ground cinnamon

1 teaspoon baking powder

1 teaspoon sea salt

1/2 teaspoon ground black pepper (optional)

INSTRUCTIONS

1. Preheat oven to 350 degrees F. Line baking pan with parchment or coat with coconut oil.
2. In large bowl, whisk eggs with hand mixer or whisk until frothy and light. Add coconut oil, sweetener and applesauce. Blend until combined.

3. Sift coconut and almond flour, chia meal, baking powder, salt and spices into wet ingredients. Beat until smooth and well combined. Stir in raisins.
4. Pour batter into prepared baking pan.
5. Bake for 20 - 25 minutes, or until golden brown and firm to the touch.
6. Remove from oven and let cool about 5 minutes.
7. Slice and serve warm. Or allow to cool completely and serve room temperature.

NOTE: Bake in oiled loaf pan for 40 - 45 minutes for **Cinnamon Raison Bread** loaf.

stevia, raw honey or agave nectar

Avocado Club Muffin

Prep Time: 10 minutes

Cook Time: 15 minutes

Servings: 12

INGREDIENTS

1 cup almond flour

2 cage-free eggs

1 avocado

4 slices nitrate-free bacon

1 tablespoon sweetener*

1 teaspoon apple cider vinegar

1 teaspoon baking powder

1/4 teaspoon ground white pepper (or black pepper)

INSTRUCTIONS

1. Preheat oven to 350 degrees F. Line muffin pan with paper liners or light coat with coconut oil. Heat medium pan over medium-high heat.

2. Finely chop bacon and add to hot pan. Sauté until crisp and cooked through, about 5 minutes. Set aside.

3. Beat eggs, sweetener and vinegar in medium mixing bowl with hand mixer or whisk until thick and slightly foamy.

4. Slice avocado in half. Scoop flesh of one half into egg mixture. Add bacon and drippings, almond flour, baking powder and black pepper and mix until combined.

5. Dice remaining avocado flesh and fold into batter.

6. Use ice cream scoop or tablespoon to scoop batter into prepared muffin pan.

7. Bake about 15 - 20 minutes, until edges are golden brown and tops are firm.

8. Remove from oven and let cool for 5 minutes.

9. Serve warm. Or cool completely and serve temperature.

NOTE: Bake in square oiled baking pan for 30 - 35 minutes for **Avocado Club Bread**.

stevia, raw honey or agave nectar

Easy Poppy Seed Muffins

Prep Time: 5 minutes

Cook Time: 20 minutes

Servings: 12

INGREDIENTS

6 eggs

1/2 cup coconut flour

1/4 cup coconut oil

1/4 cup sweetener*

1 teaspoon vanilla

1 teaspoon poppy seeds

1/2 teaspoon baking soda

Juice of 2 lemons

Zest of 2 lemons

INSTRUCTIONS

1. Preheat oven to 350 degrees F. Oil muffin pan or line with paper liners.
2. Zest, *then* juice 2 lemons. Add to large mixing bowl with eggs, coconut oil, sweetener and vanilla. Beat with hand mixer or whisk until well combined.
3. Sift coconut flour and baking soda into wet ingredients, and mix until smooth. Stir in poppy seeds.
4. Use ice cream scoop or tablespoon to pour batter into prepared muffin pan.

5. Place in oven and bake for about 20 minutes, or until golden around edges and toothpick inserted into middle comes out clean.

6. Remove from oven and let cool for 5 minutes.

7. Serve warm. Or allow to cool completely and serve room temperature.

* raw honey or agave nectar

Carrot Cake Cookie Bars

Prep Time: 10 minutes

Cook Time: 25 minutes

Servings: 12

INGREDIENTS

2 cups almond meal

2 cups shredded carrots (about 4 large carrots)

3 cage-free eggs

1/4 cup coconut oil

1/2 cup unsweetened applesauce

1/2 cup flaked coconut

1/4 cup sweetener*

2 teaspoons vanilla

2 teaspoons ground cinnamon

1 teaspoon ground nutmeg

1/2 teaspoon ground black pepper

1/2 teaspoon sea salt

INSTRUCTIONS

1. Preheat oven to 350 Degrees F. Line baking pan with parchment or coat lightly with coconut oil.
2. Grate carrots, or process in food processor or bullet blender until finely chopped. Add to medium bowl.
3. Add eggs, oil, applesauce and sweetener to food processor or bullet blender. Process until thickened and light, about 1 - 2 minutes.

4. Pour egg mixture into carrots. Sift in almond flour and salt. Add vanilla and spices. Mix well with a wooden spoon or hand mixer. Stir in coconut.

5. Press dough evenly into prepared baking pan and bake about 25 minutes, or until firm and golden brown.

6. Remove from oven and allow to cool about 10 minutes.

7. Slice into bars and serve warm. Or let cool completely and serve room temperature.

stevia, raw honey, agave nectar or maple syrup

Apple Pastries

Prep Time: 20 minutes

Cook Time: 20 minutes

Servings: 4

INSTRUCTIONS

Crust

2 cups almond flour

2 cage-free eggs

3 tablespoons coconut oil

1 tablespoon sweetener*

1/2 teaspoon baking soda

1/2 teaspoon baking powder

1 teaspoon ground cinnamon

1/4 teaspoon sea salt

Filling

2 sweet apples

1/4 cup water

1 teaspoon tapioca flour

1 tablespoon ground cinnamon

1/2 teaspoon ground nutmeg

1 teaspoon vanilla

2 tablespoons sweetener * (optional)

2 tablespoons raisins (optional)

2 tablespoons chopped walnuts (optional)

DIRECTIONS

1. For *Crust*, sift almond flour into medium mixing bowl. Add baking soda and powder, cinnamon and salt.

2. Whisk eggs and sweetener in small mixing bowl, then add to flour mixture and combine. Slowly add coconut oil until malleable dough comes together.

3. Roll in plastic wrap or wrap tightly in parchment and refrigerate for 15 minutes.

4. Preheat oven to 400 degrees. Line sheet pan with parchment or baking mat. Cover cutting board with parchment. Heat medium pan over medium-high heat.

5. For *Filling*, peel and dice apples. Add apples to hot pan with water, tapioca, cinnamon, nutmeg, and sweetener and spices (optional).

6. Stir and simmer for about 5 - 8 minutes, until apples are tender and thick glaze forms. Remove from heat and add raisins and chopped walnuts (optional).

7. Remove dough from refrigerator. Roll dough out on parchment covered cutting board to about 1/8 inch thick square with rolling pin. Use sharp knife or pizza cutter to cut dough into 4 squares.

8. Scoop equal portions of *Filling* into center of one side of each dough square. Fold bare half of dough over filled half. Press edges together and secure seal, letting any trapped air escape. Repeat with remaining dough.

9. Arrange pies on lined sheet pan and bake 15 - 20 minutes, or until dough is golden and cooked through.

10. Serve immediately. Or allow to cool and serve room temperature.

*stevia, raw honey or agave nectar

Orange Cranberry Muffins

Prep Time: 5 minutes

Cook Time: 20 minutes

Servings: 12

INGREDIENTS

1 1/2 cups almond flour

2 cage-free eggs

1/2 cup fresh squeezed orange juice (about 2 oranges)

1/4 cup coconut oil

1/4 cup dried cranberries

1 tablespoon orange zest

1 teaspoon baking powder

1/2 teaspoon vanilla

1/2 teaspoon sea salt

INSTRUCTIONS

1. Preheat oven to 350 degrees F. Line muffin pan with paper liners or coconut oil.
2. In medium bowl, beat eggs with hand mixer or whisk until light and a foamy. Add coconut oil, orange juice and zest. Beat well.
3. Sift in almond flour, baking powder, vanilla and salt. Mix until combined. Stir in cranberries.
4. Use ice cream scoop or tablespoon to scoop batter into prepared muffin pan.

5. Bake about 20 minutes, or until toothpick inserted into center comes out clean.

6. Remove from oven and serve warm. Or let cool completely and serve room temperature.

NOTE: Bake in oiled loaf pan for 40 - 45 minutes for **Cranberry Orange Bread**.

stevia, raw honey or agave nectar

Onion Crumpets

Prep Time: 5 minutes

Cook Time: 15 minutes

Servings: 4

INGREDIENTS

1/3 cup coconut flour

4 eggs

1/4 cup nut milk

2 tablespoons coconut oil

1 tablespoon unsweetened applesauce

1/2 teaspoon baking soda

1 teaspoon organic apple cider vinegar

1 teaspoon onion powder

1/4 teaspoon sea salt

1 teaspoon dehydrated onion flakes (optional)

INSTRUCTIONS

1. Preheat oven to 400 degrees F. Coat 4 mini-round cake pans or 4-inch diameter ramekins with coconut oil.

2. In small mixing bowl, mix baking soda and apple cider vinegar. Set aside and allow to froth.

3. In medium bowl, beat eggs with hand mixer or whisk until thick and lightened. Add flour, nut milk, applesauce, onion powder and salt. Mix to combine.

4. Add baking soda and vinegar mixture to medium bowl. Blend well until smooth.

5. Pour batter into prepared pans or ramekins and sprinkle on dehydrated onion flakes (optional). Bake for 12 - 15 minutes, until slightly golden and center is firm to the touch.

6. Remove muffins from oven. Loosen from sides of pans or ramekins with knife, then turn out.

7. Serve warm. Or let cool complete and serve room temperature.

Spinach Mushroom Muffins

Prep Time: 10 minutes

Cook Time: 15 minutes

Servings: 12

INGREDIENTS

1 cup almond flour

2 eggs

1 cup fresh spinach

1/2 cup fresh mushrooms

1 tablespoon sweetener*

1 tablespoon apple cider vinegar

1 teaspoon baking soda

1 teaspoon baking powder

1 teaspoon ground white pepper (or black pepper)

1/2 teaspoon ground nutmeg

1/2 teaspoon dried basil

INSTRUCTIONS

1. Preheat oven to 350 degrees F. Line muffin pan with paper liners or lightly coat with coconut oil. Heat medium pan over medium-high heat.

2. Slice mushrooms and add to hot pan. Sauté about 3 minutes, then add spinach. Sauté until water evaporates, mushrooms are cooked through and spinach is wilted. Set aside.

3. Beat eggs, sweetener and vinegar in medium mixing bowl with hand mixer or whisk until thick and frothy.

4. Add sautéed veggies, almond flour, baking soda and powder and spices and mix until combined.

5. Use ice cream scoop or tablespoon to pour batter into prepared muffin pan.

6. Bake 15 - 20 minutes, until edges are golden brown and tops are firm.

7. Remove muffins from oven and let cool about 5 minutes.

8. Serve warm. Or allow to cool complete and serve temperature.

NOTE: Bake in square oiled baking pan for 30 - 35 minutes for **Spinach Mushroom Bread**.

stevia, raw honey or agave nectar

Rosemary Basil Scones

Prep Time: 10 minutes

Cook Time: 25 minutes

Servings: 8

INGREDIENTS

2 cups almond flour

1/3 cup arrowroot flour

1 egg

1/4 cup organic coconut oil

1/2 lemon

2 tablespoons sweetener*

2 teaspoons baking powder

2 sprigs fresh rosemary

 5 - 6 large basil leaves (or 1 1/2 teaspoons dried basil)

1/2 teaspoon vanilla

1/2 teaspoon sea salt

1/4 cup hazelnuts (optional)

INSTRUCTIONS

1. Preheat oven to 350 degrees F. Line sheet pan with parchment or coat with coconut oil.

2. Whisk together flours, baking powder, salt and vanilla in large mixing bowl.

3. Zest 1/2 lemon into small mixing bowl. Finely chop rosemary and chiffon fresh basil. Add herbs to bowl with egg and sweetener.

Beat with hand mixer or whisk while slowly pouring in coconut oil.

4. Add egg mixture to flour blend and mix until well combined.

5. Chop and fold in hazelnuts (optional). Form dough into ball and place on sheet pan. Flatten to 1/2 inch thick circle with hands.

6. Cut into eight wedges with pizza cutter or sharp knife. Arrange at least 1 inch apart on sheet pan and bake for 20 - 25 minutes , or until edges are golden brown.

7. Remove and let cool. Serve room temperature.

orange juice, raw honey, agave nectar or maple syrup

Fennel Breakfast Biscuits

Prep Time: 5 minutes

Cook Time: 15 minutes

Servings: 8

INGREDIENTS

2 1/2 cups fine almond flour (not almond meal)

2 eggs

1/4 cup coconut oil

2 tablespoons fennel seeds

1 teaspoon baking soda

1/2 teaspoon sea salt

1 tablespoon sweetener*

INSTRUCTIONS

1. Preheat oven to 350 degrees F. Line sheet pan with parchment paper.
2. Grind 1 tablespoon fennels seeds in spice grinder or high-speed blender.
3. Combine almond flour, baking soda, salt and ground fennel in medium bowl.
4. Separate egg whites into separate medium bowl, and yolks into small bowl. Beat egg whites to soft peaks with hand mixer or whisk, about 5 minutes.
5. Mix yolks, oil and sweetener into whites. Mix egg mixture into dry ingredients to form soft, solid dough.

6. Roll dough into balls and flatten into 1 inch round biscuits with hands. Place on prepared sheet pan and brush with coconut oil. Sprinkle on whole fennel seeds.

7. Place in oven for 12 - 15 minutes, until golden and firm on top.

8. Remove from oven and serve warm.

NOTE: Oil square baking pan, gently press in dough, use knife or pizza cutter to score in 9 squares, and bake for about 25 minutes for break-away **Fennel Breakfast Pan Biscuits**.

stevia, raw honey or agave nectar

Everything Bagels

Prep Time:10 minutes

Cook Time: 25 minutes

Servings: 8

INGREDIENTS

2 cups almond flour

2 tablespoons coconut flour

4 eggs

1/3 cup apple cider vinegar

2 tablespoons sweetener*

2 tablespoons unsweetened applesauce

2 tablespoons ground chia seed (or flax meal)

1 tablespoon tapioca flour (or arrowroot powder)

1 teaspoon baking soda

1 teaspoon garlic powder

1 teaspoon onion powder

1 teaspoon poppy seeds

1 teaspoon sesame seeds

1 teaspoon caraway seeds (optional)

1/2 teaspoon sea salt

INSTRUCTIONS

1. Preheat oven to 350 degrees F. Lightly coat donut pan with
   coconut oil.

2. Add flours, chia or flax meal, baking soda and salt to food processor or high-speed blender. Process for 1 minute, until very fine.

3. Add eggs, sweetener, applesauce, vinegar, salt and spices to flour mixture. Process until fully blended, about 1 - 2 minutes.

4. Carefully scoop batter into donut pan, avoiding raised middle. Sprinkle on poppy, sesame and caraway seeds (optional).

5. Place in oven and bake for 20 - 25 minutes.

6. Remove at let cool about 5 minutes. Then remove bagels from pan.

7. Serve immediately Or let cool completely and serve room temperature.

NOTE: Bake in 8 round mini cake pans lightly coated with coconut oil if you do not have a donut pan.

stevia, raw honey or agave nectar

Avocado Banana Bread

Prep Time: 5 minutes

Cook Time: 25 minutes

Servings: 9

INGREDIENTS

3/4 cup almond flour

1/4 cup coconut flour

2 tablespoons flax meal (or ground chia seed)

2 eggs

1 large overripe banana

1 avocado

1/4 cup sweetener*

2 tablespoons coconut oil

1 tablespoon baking powder

1 tablespoon cinnamon

1 teaspoon ground ginger

1 teaspoon vanilla

1/2 teaspoon ground black pepper

1/2 teaspoon sea salt

1/2 cup organic banana chips (optional)

INSTRUCTIONS

1. Preheat oven to 350 degrees F. Coat square baking pan with coconut oil.

2. Slice avocado in half. Remove pit and scoop flesh into medium mixing bowl. Peel banana and add to bowl with eggs, sweetener, and flax or chia meal. Beat with hand mixer or whisk until well blended.

3. Sift flour, baking powder, salt and spices Into banana mixture. Mix until combined. Roughly chop banana chips and fold into batter (optional).

4. Pour batter into baking pan and bake for 20 - 25 minutes, or until browned and firm in the center.

5. Remove from oven and let cool at least 5 minutes.

6. Slice and serve warm. Or allow to cool completely and serve room temperature.

NOTE: Bake in oiled loaf pan for 35 - 45 minutes for **Avocado Banana Loaf**.

stevia, raw honey or agave nectar

Savory Spiced Pineapple Bread

Prep Time: 5 minutes

Cook Time: 20 minutes

Servings: 8

INGREDIENTS

2 cups almond flour

3 eggs

1/4 cup coconut oil

1 cup crushed pineapple (canned in juice or fresh)

1 tablespoon apple cider vinegar

2 teaspoons baking soda

2 teaspoons vanilla

2 teaspoons ground cinnamon

2 teaspoons ground ginger

1/2 teaspoon ground nutmeg

1/2 teaspoon paprika

1/2 teaspoon cayenne pepper

1 teaspoon ground white pepper (or black pepper)

1 teaspoon sea salt

1 teaspoon cardamom (optional)

1 teaspoon turmeric (optional)

INSTRUCTIONS

1. Preheat oven to 350 degrees F. Coat 2 small loaf pans with coconut oil.

2. Separate eggs. In large bowl, beats egg whites to soft peaks with hand mixer or whisk, about 5 minutes. Add yolks, crushed or blended pineapple, coconut oil and vinegar. Beat well.

3. In medium bowl, blend flour, baking soda, spices and salt. Pour flour mixture into egg mixture and mix well.

4. Pour batter into loaf pans and bake for about 25 minutes, until toothpick inserted into center comes out clean.

5. Remove oven and let cool at least 5 minutes. Insert knife around edges and remove from pan.

6. Slice and serve warm. Or let cool completely and serve room temperature.

NOTE: Bake in large oiled loaf pan for 35 - 45 minutes for **Savory Spiced Pineapple Loaf**.

Citrus Curry Spice Bread

Prep Time: 5 minutes

Cook Time: 20 minutes

Servings: 8

INGREDIENTS

2 cups almond flour

2 eggs

1/2 cup unsweetened applesauce

1/4 cup coconut oil

Juice of 1 lemon

Juice of 1 orange

1 teaspoon lemon zest

1 teaspoon orange zest

1 tablespoon apple cider vinegar

2 tablespoons baking powder

1 tablespoon vanilla

1 tablespoon curry powder

1 teaspoon ground cinnamon

1 teaspoon ground ginger

1 teaspoon ground white pepper (or black pepper)

1 teaspoon cardamom (optional)

1/ 4 cup pumpkin seeds (optional)

Pinch sea salt

INSTRUCTIONS

1. Preheat oven to 350 degrees F. Coat 2 small loaf pans with coconut oil.

2. Separate eggs. In large bowl, whisk egg whites to soft peaks with hand mixer or whisk. Add yolks, applesauce, oil, juices, zests and vinegar. Beat well.

3. In medium bowl, blend flour, baking powder, spices and salt. Stir flour mixture into egg mixture.

4. Pour batter into loaf pans and bake for 20 - 25 minutes, or until toothpick inserted into center comes out clean.

5. Let cool slightly. Insert knife around edges and remove from pan. Serve warm or room temperature.

NOTE: Bake in large oiled loaf pan for 35 - 45 minutes for **Citrus Curry Spice Loaf**.

stevia, raw honey or agave nectar

Asian Orange Muffins

Prep Time: 10 minutes

Cook Time: 15 minutes

Servings: 12

INGREDIENTS

1 1/2 cups almond flour

2 eggs

1 1/2 cups grated carrot

1/4 cup coconut oil

1/4 cup unsweetened applesauce

1/2 cup fresh squeezed orange juice

1 tablespoon orange zest

1 tablespoon grated fresh ginger

1 tablespoon ground ginger

1 teaspoon vanilla

1 teaspoon baking soda

1 teaspoon baking powder

1/2 teaspoon sea salt

INSTRUCTIONS

1. Preheat oven to 350 degrees F. Line muffin pan with paper liners
   or coconut oil.

2. Peel ginger. Grate ginger and carrots. In medium bowl beat eggs
   with hand mixer or whisk until light and a bit frothy. Add oil,

applesauce, orange juice and zest. Beat well. Fold in carrots and ginger.

3. Sift and stir in flour, baking soda and powder, spices and salt until combined.

4. Use ice cream scoop or tablespoon to scoop batter into muffin tins, about 1/2 - 3/4 full.

5. Bake 15 - 18 minutes, or until toothpick inserted into center comes out clean.

6. Serve warm or room temperature.

Sage Sausage Buns

Prep Time: 10 minutes

Cook Time: 15 minutes

Servings: 8

INGREDIENTS

8 oz uncooked natural sage sausage

3/4 cup coconut flour

4 eggs

1/4 cup unsweetened applesauce

1/4 almond milk

1 teaspoon baking powder

2 tablespoons ground sage

1 tablespoon fresh basil

1 teaspoon ground white pepper (or black pepper)

1/2 teaspoon salt

INSTRUCTIONS

1. Preheat oven to 350 degrees F. Coat muffin pan with coconut oil. Heat medium skillet over medium heat.

2. Brown sausage in skillet for about 5 minutes, until half way cooked. Set aside and reserve leftover oil.

3. While sausage browns, separate eggs. In large bowl, whisk egg whites to soft peaks with hand mixer or whisk. Add yolks, applesauce and almond milk. Mix until combined.

4. Mince basil. Sift flour, baking soda and salt into egg mixture. Add pepper, sage and basil. Stir to combine.

5. Distribute par-cooked sausage evenly into each muffin pan cup. Use ice cream scoop or spoon to scoop batter on top of sausage. Fill each cup no more than 3/4 full.

6. Baste with sausage dripping before placing in oven. Bake 15 - 20 minutes, or until tops are golden brown and firm to the touch.

7. Turn out buns onto plate. Serve warm or room temperature.

NOTE: Bake in oiled square baking pan for 30 - 40 minutes for **Sage Sausage Bread**.

"Corn" Muffins

Prep Time: 5 minutes

Cook Time: 15 minutes

Servings: 12

INGREDIENTS

1 cup almond flour

2 eggs

1/4 cup coconut oil

2 tablespoons unsweetened applesauce

1 teaspoon sweetener*

1 teaspoon organic apple cider vinegar

1 teaspoon baking powder

1/2 teaspoon ground turmeric (optional)

Pinch ground white pepper (optional)

INSTRUCTIONS

1. Preheat oven to 350 degrees F. Line muffin pan with paper liners or lightly coat with coconut oil.

2. Beat eggs in medium mixing bowl with hand mixer or whisk until thick and slightly frothy. Add oil, applesauce, sweetener, and vinegar and mix well.

3. Stir in almond meal, baking powder, and turmeric and white pepper (optional) until combined.

4. Use ice cream scoop or tablespoon to scoop batter into muffin pan, about 1/2 - 3/4 full.

5. Bake 15 - 18 minutes until edges are golden brown and the tops are firm.

6. Serve warm or room temperature.

NOTE: Bake in square oiled baking pan for 25 - 35 minutes for **"Corn"** **Bread**.

stevia, raw honey or agave nectar

Key Lime Coconut Bars

Prep Time: 15 minutes

Cook Time: 30 minutes

Servings: 12

INGREDIENTS

Crust

1/2 cup raw cashews

2/3 cup coconut flour

2 eggs

2 tablespoons coconut oil

2 tablespoons sweetener*

1 tablespoon flaked or shredded coconut

1 teaspoon fresh lime juice

1/2 teaspoon baking soda

1/2 teaspoon vanilla

Filling

2 eggs

2 egg yolks

1 cup fresh key lime juice or (about 12 key limes - sub 10 Persian limes)

1/2 cup sweetener*

1/3 - 1/2 cup flaked or shredded coconut

2 tablespoons coconut flour

1 teaspoon lime zest

INSTRUCTIONS

1. Preheat oven to 350 degrees F. Lightly coat rectangular baking dish with coconut oil, or line with parchment.

2. For *Crust*, add cashews and coconut to food processor or bullet blender and process until finely ground. Add remaining *Crust* ingredients to food processor and pulse until dough comes together.

3. Press dough into bottom of baking dish, and slightly up the sides. Dock crust with fork to prevent bubbling.

4. Place crust in oven and bake for 8 - 10 minutes.

5. For *Filling*, beat together eggs, egg yolks, lime juice, lime zest and sweetener with hand mixer or whisk in medium bowl.

6. Sift in coconut flour and beat to combine. Let mixture sit for 5 minutes. Add coconut and beat again.

7. Pour *Filling* over par baked crust. Place in oven and bake 20 minutes, until center is set but still jiggles slightly.

8. Remove from oven and let cool for 20 minutes. Refrigerate about 20 minutes, until fully set and chilled.

9. Serve chilled or room temperature.

* raw honey or agave nectar

Heart Healthy Lunches

Chicken Soup

Prep Time: 10 minutes

Cook Time: 40 minutes

Servings: 4

INGREDIENTS

1 large yellow onion, chopped

4 garlic cloves, minced

2 carrots, chopped

2 stalks of celery, chopped

1 cup sliced mushrooms

½ cup parsley, chopped

4 cups chicken broth

2 skinless chicken legs

2 skinless chicken thighs

2 Tablespoons olive oil

1 teaspoon sea salt

INSTRUCTIONS

1. Sauté onion and garlic in olive oil in a large stockpot over medium heat until translucent.
2. Add the celery, carrots, and mushrooms and cook, stirring, for about 5 minutes.
3. Add the chicken legs and thighs, broth, parsley, and salt. Cover and simmer for 30 minutes.

4. Remove the chicken from the pot and pull the meat off the bones. Chop the meat and add it back to the pot. Simmer another 5 minutes, then serve.

Emerald Soup

Prep Time: 10 minutes

Cook Time: 25 minutes

Servings: 4

INGREDIENTS

2 large leeks, sliced

2 Tablespoons fresh ginger, grated

4 garlic cloves, minced

2 cups Chinese cabbage, chopped

4 cups fresh spinach

4 cups chicken or vegetable broth

2 Tablespoons coconut oil

1 teaspoon sea salt

INSTRUCTIONS

1. Sauté leeks in coconut oil in a large stockpot over medium-high heat about 5 minutes.

2. Add ginger and garlic, and stir, cooking, for another minute.

3. Add the cabbage, broth, and salt. Cover, and simmer for 20 minutes.

4. Add the spinach and stir in until wilted.

Vietnamese Chicken Wraps

Prep Time: 10 minutes

Cook Time: 15 minutes

Servings: 2

INGREDIENTS

1 cup chicken stock

1 pound skinless chicken breasts

1 small head cabbage

1 large carrot, grated

½ cup mint leaves, chopped

½ cup cilantro leaves, chopped

1 cucumber, grated

1 clove garlic, chopped

2 Tbsp lime juice

2 Tbsp olive oil

INSTRUCTIONS

1. Remove 6 outer leaves from cabbage. Wash, pat dry, and put 3 on each plate. Shred the remaining cabbage.
2. In a shallow pan, poach the chicken in the stock until cooked through (about 15 minutes).
3. Allow the chicken to cool, then shred and mix with the cabbage, carrots, cucumbers, mint, cilantro, lime, garlic, and olive oil.
4. Divide the mixture between the cabbage leaves.
5. Roll up the cabbage leaves and serve.

Crab-Stuffed Avocados

Prep Time: 15 minutes

Chill Time: 30 minutes

Servings: 4

INGREDIENTS

½ pound fresh crab meat, cooked

1 small bunch chives, chopped

2 stalks celery, chopped fine

1 cucumber, peeled and diced

2 large ripe avocados

2 lemons, juiced

2 Tablespoons olive oil

1 teaspoon sea salt

INSTRUCTIONS

1. In a large bowl, mix the crab, chives, celery, and cucumber.
2. In a small bowl, whisk together the oil, half of the lemon juice, and salt. Combine with the crab mixture.
3. Halve and pit the avocados. Scoop out the avocado meat from the bottom center of each half to create a "bowl." Chop the avocado and add it to the crab.
4. Rub the remaining lemon juice on the cut surfaces of the avocados.
5. Fill each avocado half with the crab mixture.
6. Chill for about 30 minutes before serving.

Shrimp and Mango Salad

Prep Time: 10 minutes

Cook Time: 5

Servings: 2

INGREDIENTS

1 pound shrimp, cleaned, tails on

1 small red onion, thinly sliced

1 cup mango, peeled and chopped

1 avocado, peeled and chopped

4 cups mixed greens

2 Tablespoons lime juice

1 Tablespoon olive oil

1 Tablespoon coconut oil

½ cup fresh cilantro, chopped

1 teaspoon sea salt

INSTRUCTIONS

1. Sauté the shrimp in 1 Tablespoon of coconut oil in a skillet over medium-high heat until pink on both sides.
2. In a bowl, combine the onion, mango, avocado, and cilantro.
3. In a separate bowl, whisk the olive oil, lime juice, and salt.
4. Serve the salad on a bed of mixed greens, top with shrimp, and drizzle the dressing over it before serving.

Indian Egg Fried "Rice"

Prep Time: 10 minutes

Cook Time: 15 minutes

Servings: 2

INGREDIENTS

1/2 head cauliflower

4 cage-free eggs

1 small carrot

1/2 red bell pepper

1/2 yellow bell pepper

1/4 onion (yellow or white)

2 small green onions (scallions)

2 tablespoons pure fish sauce (or coconut aminos or liquid aminos)

1 tablespoon coconut aminos (or coconut vinegar or liquid aminos)

1 teaspoon raw honey (or date butter or agave)

1 teaspoon sesame oil (optional)

1 large garlic clove

1/2 piece fresh ginger

1/2 teaspoon red pepper flake

Celtic sea salt, to taste

Bacon fat or coconut oil (for cooking)

Water

INSTRUCTIONS

1. Cut cauliflower into florets and add to food processor with shredding attachment to rice. Or finely mince cauliflower. Set aside.

2. Heat medium pan or wok over high heat. Lightly coat with bacon fat or coconut oil.

3. Whisk eggs in medium mixing bowl. Set aside.

4. Remove stems, seeds and veins from bell peppers, then julienne (thinly slice). Finely dice carrot. Slice green onions. Peel and mince garlic, ginger and onion.

5. Add red pepper flakes to hot oiled pan. Sauté until just cooked fragrant, about 30 seconds. Add garlic, ginger and onion and sauté about 1 minute.

6. Add cauliflower to hot pan. Sauté about 5 minutes, until cauliflower is golden and a bit softened.

7. Add carrot, peppers and 1/2 green onions. Cook another 2 - 5 minutes, until cauliflower is cooked through. Add a few tablespoons of water and cover with lid to steam, if desired.

8. Push veggies aside and make well (opening) in center of pan. Pour whisked eggs into well in center and carefully scramble until fully cooked, about 2 minutes. Mix eggs into veggies.

9. Remove from heat and transfer to serving dish. Spprinkle remaining green onions over dish and serve hot.

Easy Mushroom Bites

Prep time: 15-20 minutes

Cook time: approx 20 minutes

Serves: 2

INGREDIENTS

1 large yellow squash

½ pound organic grass-fed ground turkey

2 tbsp extra virgin olive oil

4 baby portobella mushrooms

2 cloves garlic

2 small tomatoes

12 leaves fresh basil

12 oz organic additive-free tomato sauce

3 oz olive tapenade

INSTRUCTIONS

1. Mince the garlic and cut the yellow squash into 12 slices. Cut tomatoes into 12 slices. Slice mushrooms into 12 total slices.

2. Sautee ½ pound ground turkey in 1 tbsp extra virgin olive oil in a saucepan until no longer pink. Then add minced garlic and sautee 2-3 minutes.

3. Add 12 oz organic additive-free tomato sauce and sautee until it bubbles. Remove from heat.

4. Sautee sliced mushrooms in a pan with 1 tbsp extra virgin olive oil until light brown, about 2-3 minutes.

5. For each slice of yellow squash, layer with olive tapenade, then tomato, then meat sauce, then mushroom, then basil. Serve.

Veggie Musakhan

Prep time: 4 minutes

Cook time: 8 minutes

Servings: 4

INGREDIENTS

4 pieces grass-fed chicken thighs

1 onion

2 cloves garlic

3/4 cup sliced carrots

2 handfuls Kale greens

2 tbsp chinese five spice

2 tbsp smoked paprika

2 tbsp chipotle chili pepper powder

1 tbsp olive oil

2 tsp lemon juice

1 tbsp coconut oil

INSTRUCTIONS

1. Mince garlic and chop onion to desired size (medium strips work best). Chop carrots to 1/4" thickness. De-rib the kale and chop it coarsely, wash it and allow water to remain on the leaves. Bring 4 cups of water to a light boil.

2. Heat 1 tbsp olive oil over medium heat in a large pan. Add carrot and onion and cook for 8 minutes, stirring occasionally.

3. Meanwhile, heat 1 tbsp coconut oil over medium heat in a separate pan. Add chicken and cook for 4 minutes. Season chicken with chinese five spice, chipotle chili pepper powder and smoked paprika and turn, adding more of each spice to the other side of the chicken, cooking for another 4 minutes or until cooked through.

4. Add kale to boiling water and boil until bright green, about 5 minutes. Remove from water and let sit while the vegetables and chicken continue cooking.

5. Add everything into the pan with the vegetables and add 2 tsp lemon juice. Add minced garlic and stir for 1 minute.

6. Serve immediately.

Hearty Sweet Hunter Stew

Prep time: 15 minutes

Cook time: 3 hr 45 minutes

Serves: 6

INGREDIENTS

1 ½ lbs beef stew meat

1 onion

1 (14.5 oz) can no-salt added stewed tomatoes, undrained

¼ tsp Celtic sea salt

½ tsp ground black pepper

1 dried bay leaf

2 cups water

3 tbsp arrowroot powder

12 small sweet potatoes cut in half

30 baby-cut carrots

INSTRUCTIONS

1. Heat oven to 325 degrees. In a bowl, mix arrowroot in water and stir to a paste (if you're not using arrowroot, use 1 cup water instead). Cut the onion into 8 wedges and cut potatoes in half.

2. In ovenproof Dutch oven, mix beef, onion, tomatoes, Celtic sea salt, ground black pepper and bay leaf. Mix arrowroot-thickened water (or 1 cup water) into Dutch oven.
3. Cover and bake for 2 hours, stirring one time.
4. Stir in the potatoes and carrots. Cover and bake until beef and vegetables are tender, about 1 hr 45 min. Remove bay leaf and serve immediately, or chill 20 minutes and then serve.

All-Day Meatball Marinara

Prep Time: 20 minutes

Cook Time: 4 hours

Servings: 4

INGREDIENTS

24 oz (1 1/2 lbs) ground meat (ground beef, pork, turkey, or any combination)

1/2 cup almond meal (or finely ground almonds)

2 cage-free eggs

2 cans (15 oz) organic tomato sauce

1 can (15 oz) organic crushed tomatoes

1/4 cup nutritional yeast (optional)

1 small onion (yellow or white)

2 garlic cloves

1 bay leaf

2 sprigs fresh basil

3 teaspoons dried oregano

2 teaspoons dried parsley

1 teaspoon dried basil

1/2 teaspoon onion powder

1/2 teaspoon garlic powder

1 teaspoon Celtic sea salt

1 tablespoon coconut oil (for cooking)

1 small bunch fresh flat-leaf Italian parsley (for garnish)

INSTRUCTIONS

1. Heat large skillet over medium-high heat. Add coconut oil to hot pan.

2. Peel onion and cut in half. Finely grate one half and add to medium mixing bowl. Reserve second half. Peel and mince garlic. Add half to mixing bowl. Reserve second half.

3. Add ground meat to medium mixing bowl with 1/4 cup tomato sauce, almond meal, eggs, 1 teaspoon dried oregano, 1 teaspoon dried parsley, onion powder, garlic powder, 1/2 teaspoon salt, and nutritional yeast (optional). Mix until well combined.

4. Form mixture into medium-sized meat balls. Add to hot oiled pan in batches and brown on all sides, about 5 minute per batch. Set aside in slow cooker.

5. Finely chop remaining onions. Add to hot oiled pan with garlic. Sauté about 5 minutes.

6. Add remaining tomato sauce, crushed tomatoes, 2 teaspoons dried oregano, 1 teaspoon dried parsley, 1/2 teaspoon salt, bay leaf, and fresh torn basil leaves. Stir and bring to simmer, about 5 minutes. Pour sauce over meatballs and stir to combine.

7. Cover slow cooker with lid. Turn on to low and cook 4 - 5 hours, until meatballs are cooked through.

8. Turn off slow cooker and carefully remove lid. Transfer to serving dish.

9. For garnish, chop fresh parsley and sprinkle over dish.

10. Serve hot.

Thai Coconut Soup

Prep Time: 15 minutes

Cook Time: 25 minutes

Servings: 4

INGREDIENTS

8 oz (1/2 lb) medium shrimp

1 can (13.5 oz) full-fat coconut milk

1/2 lb shiitake mushrooms (about 1 pint)

2 lemongrass stalks

2 tablespoons raw honey (or agave or date butter)

2 tablespoons lime juice

3 teaspoons pure fish sauce

5 kaffir lime leaves

1/2 inch piece ginger

1/2 teaspoon curry powder

1/2 green onion (scallion)

1/2 teaspoon red pepper flakes

Water

INSTRUCTIONS

1. Bring medium pot of salted water to a boil over high heat.
2. Peel and devein shrimp. Add to boiling water and cook about 1 minute. Drain shrimp and set aside.
3. Place pot back over high heat. Add coconut milk and 2 cups water and bring to a simmer.

4. Thinly slice ginger. Bruise lemongrass between palms, then chop. Tear lime leaves in half. Add to pot and simmer for 10 minutes.

5. Strain liquid and add back to pot. Slice mushrooms and add to pot. Simmer for 5 minutes.

6. Stir in lime juice, fish sauce, honey and curry powder. Add shrimp back to pot until heated through, about 5 minutes.

7. Transfer to serving dish. Thinly slice green onions. Sprinkle green onions and red pepper flakes over dish.

8. Serve hot.

Turkey Bacon Club Salad

Prep Time: 10 minutes

Cook Time: 5 minutes

Servings: 1

INGREDIENTS

Salad:

4 slices turkey bacon

1 tablespoon coconut oil

1 heart of romaine lettuce

2 medium tomatoes, chopped

Dressing:

1 avocado

1/2 small white onion

1 small garlic clove

Juice of 1 lemon

Small bunch of parsley leaves

Pinch sea salt

Pinch ground black pepper

INSTRUCTIONS

1. Heat medium skillet to medium-high heat and add coconut oil.
2. Chop turkey bacon and add to skillet. Browned for 2 - 3 minutes on each side, until thoroughly cooked. Remove turkey bacon and preserve any leftover oil.

3. Rinse and dry heart of romaine, then chop. Dice tomato and toss with lettuce in large bowl.

4. For ***Dressing***, slice avocado in half, pit, and spoon flesh into food processor or bullet blender. Add peeled onion and garlic, lemon juice and parsley. Add excess coconut oil from pan. Process until smooth. Salt and pepper to taste.

5. Use tongs to transfer lettuce and tomatoes to plate. Sprinkle on turkey bacon, and drizzle with avocado ***Dressing***. Serve immediately.

Beef and Plantain Stir-Fry

Prep Time: 10 minutes

Cook Time: 15 minutes

Servings: 2

INGREDIENTS

8 oz grass-fed beef

1 sweet plantain

1 small yellow onion

1/2 red bell pepper

2 cloves garlic

1 Serrano pepper

1 teaspoon ground cumin

1 teaspoon chili powder

1 teaspoon paprika

Small bunch fresh cilantro

1/2 lime

Coconut oil (for cooking)

INSTRUCTIONS

1. Bring a medium pot to boil with lightly salted water. Leave enough room in pot for sweet plantain. Heat large skillet over high medium heat and coat with coconut oil.

2. To peel plantain, cut in half then careful make at least 4 slices through peel lengthwise. Get finger or butter knife under tough peel and pry off.

3. Cut peeled plantain cut into 1 inch pieces, then in half, forming half moons. Add to boiling water for about 5 - 8 minutes, or until tender but not mushy.

4. Stem and seed peppers. Peel onion and garlic. Dice beef into half inch cubes and add to medium bowl. Mince Serrano pepper and garlic, and add to beef. Sprinkle with cumin, chili powder and paprika. Mix with wooden spoon to avoid getting hot pepper oil on skin.

5. Slice onion and bell pepper and add to hot skillet. Sauté about 1 minute. Add seasoned beef to skillet. Sauté another 2 minutes to brown.

6. Remove plantains from boiling water and drain. Add to hot skillet and stir-fry all together for about 2 - 3 minutes, until beef is browned and cook to about medium-well and plantains are a bit caramelized.

7. Chop fresh cilantro. Remove skillet from heat and toss stir-fry with cilantro. Plate stir-fry and squeeze over lime juice. Serve hot.

Tuna Spread

Prep Time: 5 minutes

Servings: 1

INGREDIENTS

7oz (1 can) chunk light tuna

1 avocado

1/2 small red Onion

1 carrot

1 celery stalk

1/2 Lemon

1/2 cucumber

Ground black pepper, to taste

sea salt, to taste

Paprika, to taste

INSTRUCTIONS

1. Drain tuna. Cut celery stalk in half, and preserve larger end. Peel onion. Slice avocado in half, pit and scoop out flesh into small bowl. Mash well.
2. Finely dice onion, smaller half of celery stalk, and carrot. Add to bowl, with spices to taste.
3. Add tuna to bowl, plus squeeze of lemon. Mix until combined and smooth.
4. Slice reserved half of celery stalk into sticks. Slice cucumber into 1/3 inch round.

5. Serve tuna in bowl with cucumber chips and celery sticks.

Healthy Chicken Pot Pie

Prep Time: 15 minutes

Cook Time: 30 minutes

Servings: 4

INGREDIENTS

Filling

8 oz skin-on chicken

1 1/2 cup chicken broth

2 tablespoons tapioca flour

2 tablespoons coconut oil

2 carrots

1 celery stalk

1 green bell pepper

1 small onion

2 garlic cloves

2 teaspoons dried thyme (or 4 teaspoons fresh thyme)

1 tablespoon lemon juice

1/2 teaspoon black pepper

Pinch sea salt

Crust

1/3 cup almond flour

2 tablespoons coconut flour

3 tablespoons cold coconut oil (or cacao butter)

1 egg

3 - 4 teaspoons water

1/2 teaspoon dried thyme

1/4 teaspoon sea salt

INSTRUCTIONS

1. Preheat oven to 400 degrees F. Heat medium pot over medium heat.

2. Add two tablespoon coconut oil to hot pot. Add chicken pieces skin side down. Cook about 3 minutes, then turn with tongs and continue cooking another 3 minutes. Remove chicken and set aside.

3. Whisk coconut flour into pot until smooth. Gradually whisk in chicken broth. Simmer about 5 minutes, whisking occasionally.

4. Peel and mince garlic. Chop carrots, celery, onion and bell pepper. Add to pot with thyme, salt pepper and lemon juice.

5. Chop par-cooked chicken meat. Add back to pot and simmer for 5 minutes. Remove from heat and set aside.

6. For *Crust*, add cold coconut oil to flours, thyme and salt in small bowl. Cut fat into flour with fork until crumbly. Mix in egg and enough water to bring together tender dough.

7. Divide dough into 4 portions. Roll into balls and flatten into round disks large enough to fit over mini pie tins or ceramic ramekins with hand, then rolling pin.

8. Pour *Filling* into vessels and cover with crusts. Pinch edges of dough over edges of vessels to seal in liquid. Brush top of each pie with coconut oil, coconut milk, or egg wash and sprinkle with salt. Use knife to cut a slit in the top of each pie.

9. Bake pot pies for about 15 minutes, until crust is golden.

10. Remove from oven and allow pies to cool for 10 minutes.

11. Serve warm. Or let cool completely and serve room temperature.

Asian Empanada

Prep Time: 20 minutes

Cook Time: 20 minutes

Servings: 4

INSTRUCTIONS

Crust

1 cup almond flour

1 cup coconut flour

2 eggs

3 tablespoons sesame oil (or coconut oil)

1/2 teaspoon garlic powder

1/2 teaspoon onion powder

1/2 teaspoon ground ginger

1/4 teaspoon baking soda

1 teaspoon sea salt

1 tablespoon sesame oil (or coconut oil)

1 tablespoon sesame seeds

Filling

6 oz chicken or shrimp

1/2 head cabbage (1 cup shredded)

1 carrot

1/4 cup mushrooms

2 inch piece fresh ginger

2 garlic cloves

1 tablespoon pure fish sauce

1 teaspoon apple cider vinegar

1 shallot

1 scallion

1 teaspoon sesame oil

DIRECTIONS

1. For *Crust*, sift almond and coconut flour into medium mixing bowl. Add baking soda, spices and salt.
2. Whisk eggs in small mixing bowl, then add to flour and combine. Slowly add 3 tablespoons oil until malleable dough comes together.
3. Roll in plastic wrap or wrap tightly in parchment and refrigerate for 15 minutes.
4. Preheat oven to 400 degrees. Line sheet pan with parchment or baking mat. Cover cutting board with parchment. Het medium pan over medium heat.
5. Shred cabbage, grate carrot, slice mushrooms. Peel and grate ginger. Slice scallion. Peel and mince shallot and garlic. Dice chicken or slice shrimp in half.
6. Add sesame oil to pan. Add chicken or shrimp hot oiled pan with ginger, shallot and garlic. Sauté about 90 seconds. Add cabbage, carrot, and mushrooms and sauté for a minute.
7. Add vinegar and fish sauce. Sauté about 3 minutes until cabbage is wilted. Stir in scallions. Remove from heat and set aside.
8. Remove dough from refrigerator. Divide dough into 4 portions. Roll dough into balls and flatten on parchment covered cutting

board with hands. Roll into circles about 1/8 inch thick with rolling pin.

9. Scoop equal portions of *Filling* into center of one side of dough circle. Fold bare half of dough over filled half. Press edges together, letting any trapped air escape. Crimp edges of dough together with fork. Repeat with remaining dough.

10. Bruch tops of empanada with sesame oil and sprinkle with sesame seeds.

11. Arrange empanadas on lined sheet pan and bake 15 - 20 minutes, or until dough is golden and cooked through.

12. Serve immediately. Or allow to cool and store in air-tight container.

Stewed Chicken and Dumplings

Prep Time: 10 minutes

Cook Time: 1 hour 20 minutes

Servings: 4

INGREDIENTS

2 lb whole chicken (innards removed)

6 - 10 cups water

3 carrots

3 celery stalks

1 small white onion (or yellow onion)

4 bay leaves

1 1/2 tablespoons dried thyme (or 4 sprigs fresh thyme)

1/2 teaspoon dried oregano

1 teaspoon paprika

2 teaspoon ground black pepper

1 tablespoon Celtic sea salt

Dumplings

3 cups almond flour

1/2 cup arrowroot powder

2 cage-free egg

1/2 cup coconut oil, chilled (or coconut or cacao butter, room temperature)

1/2 teaspoon baking soda

1/4 teaspoon ground bay leaf

1 teaspoon dried thyme

1/2 teaspoon ground white pepper (or ground black pepper)

1 teaspoon Celtic sea salt

Nut milk (or chicken broth or stock)

INSTRUCTIONS

1. Heat large pot over medium-high heat. Place chicken breast-down in hot pot. Sear chicken and turn to brown and render out fat for about 15 minutes.

2. Chop carrots and celery. Peel onion and mince. Add to chicken with salt and spices. Sauté about 2 minutes.

3. Add enough water to pot to cover chicken. Increase heat to high and bring to a boil. Reduce heat to medium and simmer about 30 minutes. Place lid loosely over pot to prevent splatter, if necessary.

4. For *Dumplings*, sift almond flour and arrowroot into medium mixing bowl. Cut in solid oil or butter with fork until crumbly mixture forms. Add egg, salt and spices, baking soda, and enough nut milk or chicken broth from pot to bring together soft, slightly sticky dough.

5. Carefully remove chicken from pot with long utensil and set aside. Use utensils to remove skin from chicken. Carve chicken into desired pieces and place back in back.

6. Use spoon or scoop to gently drop dough into pot. Cover with well fitting lid and let simmer about 15 - 20 minutes, until *Dumplings* and chicken are cooked through. Gently stir soup to periodically prevent *Dumplings* from sticking. Turn over any *Dumplings* that are not submerged.

7. Remove from heat and transfer to serving dish. Serve hot.

Kelp Noodle Stir-Fry

Prep Time: 10 minutes

Cook Time: 10 minutes

Servings: 2

INSTRUCTIONS

1 (12 oz) package kelp noodles

8 oz grass-fed beef

1/2 sweet onion

1 red bell pepper

1 hot chili pepper

2 cloves garlic

1 inch piece fresh ginger

1/2 teaspoon paprika

1/2 teaspoon ground black pepper

1/4 teaspoon sea salt

Small bunch fresh cilantro

1 lime

Coconut oil (for cooking)

DIRECTIONS

1. Heat large skillet or medium cast-iron wok over high heat. Drain and rinse kelp noodles. Add to medium bowl and soak for 5 minutes in water and juice of 1/2 lime.

2. Stem and seed peppers. Peel onion, garlic and ginger. Dice beef into strips and add to medium mixing bowl. Mince chili pepper,

garlic and ginger. Add to beef with salt, pepper, paprika and 1 teaspoon coconut oil. Mix with wooden spoon to evenly coat beef.

3. Slice onion and bell pepper and add to hot skillet. Sauté about 2 minutes. Add seasoned beef to skillet and sauté another 2 minutes to brown.

4. Drain kelp noodles and add to skillet. Stir until beef is browned and cooked to about medium-well, kelp noodles are heated through, and veggies caramelize.

5. Remove skillet from heat and plate stir-fry. Chop fresh cilantro.

6. Top stir-fry with cilantro and squeeze of 1/2 lime.

7. Serve hot.

Quick Chili

Prep Time: 5 minutes

Cook Time: 20 minutes

Servings: 4

INGREDIENTS

1 lb lean grass-fed ground beef (or elk, bison, turkey or chicken)

15 oz (1 can) organic tomato sauce

6 oz (1 can) organic tomato paste

1 small onion

1 bell pepper

2 cloves garlic

2 tablespoons chili powder

1 tablespoon ground cumin

1 tablespoon smoked paprika (or paprika)

1 teaspoon Mexican oregano (or dried oregano)

1 teaspoon ground black pepper

1 teaspoon sea salt

1/2 teaspoon cayenne pepper

1 tablespoon coconut oil

sea salt, to taste

INSTRUCTIONS

1. Heat medium pot over medium-high heat. Add 1 tablespoon
   coconut oil.

2. Peel onion and garlic. Stem and seed bell pepper. Chop and add to food processor or bullet blender. Pulse until finely minced.

3. Add to skillet and sauté for about 1 minute. Add ground beef and spices. Brown beef for about 5 minutes. Stir with whisk to break up meat well, or wooden spoon to keep beef chunkier.

4. Add whole cans of tomato sauce and paste. Stir to combine.

5. Bring to a simmer, then reduce heat to medium and cover loosely with lid to prevent splatter. Simmer about 10 minutes. Stir occasionally.

6. Use large serving spoon or ladle to serve hot.

Veggie Burger

Prep Time: 5 minutes

Cook Time: 20 minutes

Servings: 4

INGREDIENTS

Soft Burger Bun

Veggie Burger

2 eggs

1/2 head cauliflower

2 medium carrots

1 small white onion

1 cup walnuts (1/2 cup ground)

1/4 cup almond flour

2 tablespoons tapioca flour

2 tablespoons ground chia seed (or flax meal)

2 cloves garlic

1 teaspoon paprika

1 teaspoon ground black pepper

1 teaspoon sea salt

Topping

1 avocado

1 heirloom tomato

1 white onion

2 ribs romaine lettuce (or preferred lettuce)

INSTRUCTIONS

1. Preheat oven to 350 degrees F. Line sheet pan with parchment paper, or lightly coat with coconut oil. Or lightly coat 6 mini round cake pans with coconut oil.
2. Prepare *Soft Burger Buns* and place in oven.
3. While bread bakes, line dish with parchment paper.
4. Add walnuts and almond four to food processor or bullet blender. Process until finely ground. Add to medium mixing bowl.
5. Peel small onion and garlic. Add to processor or blender with cauliflower and carrots. Process until finely ground. Add eggs, tapioca and chia. Process until mixture becomes thickened and has batter-like consistency.
6. Add veggie mixture and spices to mixing bowl. Mix all ingredients together with hands or wooden spoon until fully combined and uniform.
7. Form veggie mixture into 4 patties and place on parchment lined dish. Place in freezer for 10 minutes.
8. Heat medium skillet over medium-high heat and add 1 tablespoon coconut oil.
9. Peel onion. Make 4 thick slices, keeping full ring intact. Using spatula, place full rings into hot oiled pan. Sear 1 minute on each side. Set aside on paper towel to drain.
10. Reduce heat to medium and coat pan with coconut oil.
11. Remove veggie patties from freezer and place in hot oiled pan. Cook 5 minutes, then carefully flip with spatula and cook another 5 minutes.

12. Remove *Soft Burger Bun* from oven and let cool about 5 minutes.

13. Cut lettuce ribs in half. Cut tomato into 4 thick slices. Slice avocado in half, pit and slice flesh in peel.

14. Slice bun in half and place lettuce on bottom bun, followed by tomato slice. Add burger patty, then grilled onion ring. Finish with a few slices of avocado and top bun.

15. Serve immediately.

Kelp Noodle Salad

Prep Time: 5 minutes

Cook Time: 5 minutes

Servings: 2

INGREDIENTS

1 package (12 oz) kelp noodles

1/2 lemon

1 small cucumber

1 small red bell pepper

1 large carrot

Small bunch cilantro

2 large basil leaves

Orange Avocado Dressing

1 avocado

1 large orange

1/2 lemon

5 large basil leaves

1/4 teaspoon ground black pepper

1/4 teaspoon cayenne pepper or red pepper flake (optional)

Large bunch cilantro

INSTRUCTIONS

1. Rinse and drain kelp noodles. Add to medium bowl and soak 5
   minutes in warm water and juice of 1/2 lemon. Or bring medium pot

of water with juice of 1/2 lemon to a boil and cook kelp noodles for 5 minutes, if softer texture preferred.

2. Peel, seed and cut cucumber in half width-wise. Cut bell pepper in half, then remove stem, seeds and veins. Use vegetable peeler or grater to make long, thin slices of carrot. Thinly slice cucumber and bell pepper lengthwise.

3. Add veggies and drained kelp noodles to medium mixing bowl.

4. For *Orange Avocado Dressing*, add basil and cilantro leaves to food processor or bullet blender with juice of orange and process to break down leaves. Slice avocado in half and remove pit. Scoop flesh into processor with juice of 1/2 lemon, black pepper and hot pepper (optional). Process until thick and until creamy.

5. Pour *Orange Avocado Dressing* over sliced veggies and kelp noodles. Toss to coat.

6. Serve immediately. Or refrigerate for 20 minutes and serve chilled.

Simple Gazpacho + Tortilla Chips

Prep Time: 20 minutes

Cook Time: 10 minutes

Servings: 4

INGREDIENTS

Grain-Free Tortillas (recipe below)

Gazpacho

2 (11.5 oz) cans organic tomato juice (or 3 cups juiced tomatoes)

4 plum tomatoes

2 red bell peppers

1 red onion

1 cucumber

3 garlic cloves

1/4 cup apple cider vinegar

1/4 cup coconut oil (or 2 tablespoons coconut oil and 2 tablespoons flavorful oil [walnut, almond, sesame, etc.])

1 teaspoon cracked black pepper (or ground black pepper)

1/2 tablespoon sea salt

INSTRUCTIONS

1. Seed cucumber and tomatoes. Seed, stem and vein bell peppers. Peel onion and garlic. Dice veggies, mince garlic, and add to medium serving bowl.

2. Add tomato juice, vinegar, oil, salt and pepper, and mix well. Place in refrigerator.

3. Heat medium pan over medium-high heat and coat with coconut oil.

4. For *Tortilla Chips*, prepare *Grain-Free Tortillas*.

5. Add more coconut oil to hot pan and allow to heat up. Cut tortillas into wedges with pizza cutter or sharp knife.

6. Add tortilla wedges back to hot pan in single layer and cook about 30 seconds on each side, until golden and crisp. Drain on paper towel. Repeat with remaining tortilla wedges.

7. Transfer warm *Tortilla Chips* to serving dish. Serve immediately with chilled *Gazpacho*.

Shrimp Taco

Prep Time: 15 minutes

Cook Time: 20 minutes

Servings: 4

INGREDIENTS

Grain-Free Tortillas (recipe below)

Filling

12 oz medium shrimp

1/2 small red onion

1 fresh jalapeño or (2 oz pickled jalapeño)

1 garlic clove

1/2 inch piece ginger root

1/4 head cabbage (1 cup shredded)

Large bunch cilantro

1 avocado

1 tomato

2 limes

Coconut oil (for cooking)

INSTRUCTIONS

1. Heat large pan over medium-high heat and lightly coat with coconut oil.
2. Prepare *Grain-Free Tortillas*, with 4 smaller portions.

3. Keep tortillas warm and moist in oven set to WARM under damp paper towel.

4. Use clean paper towel to carefully wipe out pan. Add 1 tablespoon coconut oil to pan.

5. Peel and devein shrimp, and remove tail. Peel and mince garlic and ginger. Peel and thinly slice onion. Slice fresh jalapeños.

6. Add shrimp to pan with garlic, ginger, onion and jalapeños. Sauté about 2 minutes, then squeeze juice of 1 lime and sprinkle pinch of salt and pepper over shrimp.

7. Sauté shrimp until just cooked, about 5 minutes. Remove from heat.

8. Grate radish, shred cabbage, dice tomato. Slice avocado in half, remove pit, and slice flesh in peel. Chop cilantro.

9. Remove tortillas from oven and layer with sautéed shrimp and onions. Top with shredded cabbage, radish, tomato and avocado slices. Finish with large pinch of cilantro and squeeze of lime.

10. Fold tortillas and serve warm.

Grain-Free Tortillas

Prep Time: 5 minutes

Cook Time: 10 minutes

Servings: 2

INGREDIENTS

2 tablespoons almond flour

2 tablespoons coconut flour

1/2 tablespoon flax meal (or ground chia seed)

2 eggs

1/4 cup water (plus extra)

2 tablespoons coconut oil

1/4 teaspoon baking powder

Coconut oil (for cooking)

INSTRUCTIONS

1. Heat medium frying pan over medium-high heat and coat with coconut oil.

2. Whisk together eggs, coconut oil and 1/4 cup water in medium bowl.

3. In separate mixing bowl, blend coconut flour, almond flour, flax or chia seed, and baking powder.

4. Slowly whisk as you pour flourmixture into wet ingredients. If batter appears too thick to spread fairly thin in pan, add up to 4 tablespoon water 1 tablespoon at a time.

5. Use ladle or dry measure cup to pour 1/2 of batter into hot oiled pan. Tilt pan in circular motion as you pour so batter spreads thinly.

6. Cook batter for about 2 minutes or until slightly golden and firm. Flip tortilla with tongs or spatula and cook another 2 minutes. Remove and place on paper towel or parchment.

7. Cook remaining batter for 2 minutes on each side. Re-oil pan as necessary.

8. Fill warm tortillas with meat or veggies of choice and serve warm.

Zucchini Salad with Sundried Tomato Sauce

Prep Time: 20 minutes*

Servings: 2

INGREDIENTS

1 medium zucchini

1 tomato

5 sundried tomatoes

1 garlic clove

2 fresh basil leaves

1 tablespoon raw virgin coconut oil (or 2 tablespoons warm water)

1/4 teaspoon ground white pepper (or black pepper)

1/4 teaspoon sea salt

INSTRUCTIONS

1. Run zucchini through spiralizer, slice into long, thin shreds with knife, or use vegetable peeler to make flat, thin slices. Sprinkle with a pinch of salt and pepper, and gently toss to coat.

2. Add tomato, sundried tomatoes, peeled garlic, basil, coconut oil or warm water, and remaining salt and pepper to food processor or bullet blender. Process until sauce of desired consistency forms.

3. Transfer zucchini pasta to serving bowls. Top with tomato sauce and serve immediately.

4. Or refrigerate for 20 minutes and serve chilled.

Spicy Tuna Tartare

Prep Time: 15* minutes

Servings: 4

INGREDIENTS

1 lb tuna steak (sushi grade)

1 small cucumber

1 ripe avocado

1 lime

1 garlic clove

1 hot chile pepper

2 tablespoons raw virgin coconut oil

Small bunch fresh cilantro

1 teaspoon red pepper flake

1 teaspoon sea salt

INSTRUCTIONS

1. Peel, seed and dice cucumber and avocado. Finely chop cilantro. Add to medium mixing bowl.

2. Remove seeds, stem and veins from hot pepper. Peel garlic and add to food processor or bullet blender with cayenne and hot pepper. Process until smooth paste forms. Add to bowl.

3. Dice tuna, discarding any tough white gristle. Add to bowl.

4. Squeeze on lime juice and add salt.

5. Gently toss with soft spatula or large spoon.

6. Serve immediately. Or refrigerate 20 minutes and serve chilled.

Almond Cheese and Nori

Prep Time: 15 minutes*

Servings: 2

INGREDIENTS

1 cup raw almonds*

1/4 cup water

2 tablespoons coconut oil

1 tablespoon lemon juice

1 tablespoon raw apple cider vinegar

1 garlic clove

1/4 teaspoon paprika

1/4 teaspoon ground black pepper

1/2 teaspoon sea salt

4 - 6 sheets dried nori (seaweed paper)

INSTRUCTIONS

1. *For *Almond Cheese*, soak almonds in enough water to cover overnight. Drain and rinse. Pop off skins and discard.

2. Add soaked almonds, water, coconut oil, lemon juice, vinegar, peeled garlic, salt and spices to food processor or bullet blender and process until smooth. Add a few extra tablespoons of water if necessary to achieve thick but smooth consistency. Transfer *Almond Cheese* to serving dish.

3. Cut nori into small sheets and serve with *Almond Cheese*.

Mango Ginger Apple Salad

Prep Time: 5 minutes

Servings: 2

INSTRUCTIONS

1 ripe mango

1 granny smith apple

1/4 cup raw cashews

1 inch piece fresh ginger

1/2 teaspoon ground ginger

INGREDIENTS

1. Slice mango in half around pit. Peel flesh and dice. Add to small mixing bowl.
2. Core apple and dice. Peel ginger and mince. Add to bowl with ground ginger.
3. Roughly chop cashews and add to bowl.
4. Mix well and serve immediately. Or refrigerate 20 minutes and serve chilled.

Raspberry Almond Salad

Prep Time: 10 minutes

Servings: 1

INGREDIENTS

Salad

2 cups soft lettuce leaves (looseleaf or butterhead varieties)

1/2 cup watercress

2 tablespoons raw almonds (slivered or sliced)

1/4 cup fresh raspberries

Raspberry Vinaigrette

1/4 cup raspberries (fresh or frozen)

2 tablespoons lemon juice (or raw apple cider vinegar)

2 tablespoons raw walnuts (or raw walnut oil, coconut oil, almond oil, etc.)

1 teaspoon sweetener* (optional)

Water

INSTRUCTIONS

1. For *Salad*, rinse, dry and plate lettuce and watercress. Sprinkle almonds and fresh raspberries over greens.

2. For *Raspberry Vinaigrette*, add raspberries, lemon juice, walnuts or oil, and sweetener (optional) to food processor or high-speed blender and process until smooth, about 1 minute. Add enough water to reach desired consistency.

3. Drizzle *Raspberry Vinaigrette* over salad and serve immediately.

stevia, raw honey or dried dates

Smoked Salmon Avocado Salad

Prep Time: 10 minutes

Servings: 1

INGREDIENTS

Salad

2 cups soft lettuce leaves (looseleaf or butterhead varieties)

1/2 cup watercress or dandelion leaves (optional)

2 oz smoked salmon

1/2 avocado

1 sprig fresh dill

1 tablespoon caviar (optional)

Avocado Cream Dressing

1/2 avocado

1 sprig fresh dill

1 tablespoon lemon juice

1/2 teaspoon ground black pepper

1/2 teaspoon Celtic sea salt

1/2 coconut

Water

INSTRUCTIONS

1. For *Salad*, rinse, dry and plate lettuce and watercress or dandelion leaves (optional). Cut avocado in half and remover pit. Dice or

slice avocado flesh in peel, then scoop onto greens. Lay smoked salmon over greens.

2. For *Avocado Cream Dressing*, remove coconut flesh from peel and add to food processor or high-speed blender with enough water to reach desired consistency. Process until smooth and creamy, about 1 - 2 minutes. Strain mixture through nut milk bag and place back into blender.

3. Scoop remaining avocado flesh into blender. Add lemon juice, 1 sprig dill, salt and pepper and process until well combined and smooth, about 1 minute.

4. Drizzle *Avocado Cream Dressing* over salad. Mince remaining dill and sprinkle over salad. Dollop caviar over salad (optional).

5. Serve immediately.

stevia, raw honey or dried dates

Fresh Sashimi Bento Bowl

Prep Time: 20 minutes*

Servings: 1

INGREDIENTS

2 fresh sea scallops (sushi grade)

2 oz fresh salmon filet (sushi grade)

2 oz fresh tuna filet (sushi grade)

1/2 small cucumber

1/2 avocado

1 sheet nori (dried seaweed/sushi paper)

1/2 lemon

1 oz pickled ginger (or 2 inch piece fresh ginger + 2 tablespoons raw apple cider vinegar and 1 tablespoons raw honey)

1 teaspoon real wasabi (or 2 tablespoons fresh ground horseradish)

1/2 teaspoon raw sesame seeds

2 tablespoons salmon roe or caviar (optional)

Sashimi Sauce

2 teaspoons raw sesame oil (or coconut, walnut, almond oil, etc.)

2 teaspoons coconut aminos (or tamari)

1 - 2 teaspoons raw honey

1/2 small scallion

1/2 piece ginger root

INSTRUCTIONS

1. *For fresh pickled ginger, peel ginger and use mandolin, vegetable peeler or slicing attachment on food processor to thinly slice. Add to glass container with vinegar and honey and refrigerate 1 - 7 days.

2. Have fish monger clean and filet tuna and salmon, and remove skin.

3. Place salmon, tuna and scallops in freezer for about 15 minutes to firm.

4. For sashimi sauce, peel ginger and mince. Slice scallion. Add to small mixing bowl with oil, coconut aminos and honey. Transfer to small serving bowl and set aside.

5. Use spiralizer, mandolin or vegetable peeler to thinly slice cucumber, and arrange around serving dish. Cut avocado in half and slice pitted half in peel. Scoop flesh onto serving dish beside fish.

6. Place pickled ginger and wasabi or horse around serving dish.

7. Slice lemon and cut nori into thin strips. Place around serving dish. Place salmon roe or caviar around serving dish (optional).

8. Remove fish from freezer and thinly slice. Arrange fish in center of serving dish. Serve immediately.

Spicy Chicken Wraps

Prep time: 5 minutes

Cook time: 3 minutes

INGREDIENTS

4 slices of chicken deli meat

1 tbsp olive oil

1 small onion

1 red bell pepper

1 avocado

¼ tsp garlic powder

INSTRUCTIONS

1. Remove the nut from the avocado and mash it into a paste. Chop the pepper and onion into small pieces.

2. Combine the garlic powder, pepper and onion in the bowl with the avocado and mix well.

3. Add the olive oil in a pan over low heat and heat the chicken mildly, turning frequently, for 3 minutes.

4. Remove the chicken from heat and place ¼ of the avocado/pepper/onion mixture onto each piece.

5. Wrap the chicken up into tubes and serve.

Chopped Spicy Zucchini

Prep time: 10 minutes

Cook time: 15 minutes

INGREDIENTS

6 cage-free eggs

2 handfuls spinach

2 cloves garlic

1 small zucchini

1 small yellow squash

1 tbsp extra virgin olive oil

¼ tsp Celtic sea salt

¼ tsp ground black pepper

¼ tsp thyme

INSTRUCTIONS

1. Crack eggs into a bowl and mix them with thyme. Mince garlic, chop zucchini and yellow squash half-moon slices.

2. Heat oil in a frying pan over medium heat. Sauté garlic, zucchini and yellow squash for 4 minutes, stirring occasionally.

3. Add spinach and wilt, covered, for 1 minute.

4. Pour eggs over top, cover, and reduce to low heat. Cook through, about 10 minutes. Remove from pan and sprinkle Celtic sea salt and ground black pepper over the top.

Uptown Clam Chowder

Prep Time: 10 minutes

Cook Time: 1 hour 15 minutes

Servings: 4

INGREDIENTS

24 - 36 medium live littleneck clams (or other clam varieties)

2 cans (11.5) organic tomato juice (or about 6 large tomatoes)

2 cans (14.5 oz) organic crushed tomatoes

2 medium carrots

2 medium celery stalks

2 medium parsnips

1 red bell pepper

1 tablespoon tamari (or coconut aminos or liquid aminos)

1 bay leaf

1/4 teaspoon cayenne pepper

1/2 teaspoon onion powder

1 tablespoon dried oregano

1 tablespoon dried basil

1 teaspoon dried thyme

1 teaspoon ground black pepper

Celtic sea salt, to taste

1 cup clam juice (or veggie or chicken stock, or water) (optional)

INSTRUCTIONS

1. Have fishmonger shuck clams. Or carefully shuck clams yourself. Reserve clam juice. Set aside in refrigerator.

2. Juice tomatoes, if using. Add tomato juice and crushed tomatoes to medium pot. Heat pot over high heat.

3. Remove seeds, stems and veins from bell pepper. Dice bell pepper, carrot, celery, and parsnips. Add to pot with spices and salt, to taste.

4. Bring pot to boil, then reduce heat to low. Place lid loosely over pot to prevent splatter. Simmer for 45 minutes. Stir occasionally.

5. Remove lid and stir. Add clam juice, stock or water to reach desired consistency (optional).

6. Remove clams from refrigerator and chop, if desired. Add clams and juice to pot. Stir to combine.

7. Replace lid and continue cooking about 20 - 30 minutes. Stir occasionally.

8. Transfer to serving dish and serve hot.

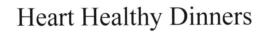
Heart Healthy Dinners

Cashew Chicken Satay

Prep Time: 10 minutes*

Cook Time: 25 minutes

Servings: 4

INGREDIENTS

16 oz (1 lb) boneless skinless chicken

12 wooden skewers (soaked in water for 1 hour)

Marinade

1 tablespoon pure fish sauce (or liquid aminos or coconut Aminos)

2 inch piece fresh ginger root

1 garlic clove

Satay Sauce

13 oz (1 can) full-fat coconut milk

1/2 cup crunchy almond butter

1 tablespoon raw honey or agave nectar

1 tablespoon pure fish sauce (or tamari or coconut aminos)

1 teaspoon apple cider vinegar (or liquid aminos or coconut vinegar)

4 shallots

2 garlic cloves

2 inch piece fresh ginger root

2 small red chili peppers

1 1/2 tablespoons lime juice

Coconut oil (for cooking)

INSTRUCTIONS

1. *Cut chicken into 1 inch strips. For *Marinade*, peel and mince garlic and ginger. Add to medium mixing bowl with fish sauce and whisk. Add chicken and toss with until coated. Cover and set aside to marinate for 1 hour.

2. *Soak wooden skewers in water in shallow dish for 1 hour.

3. Heat medium pan or wok over medium heat and add 1 tablespoon coconut oil.

4. For *Satay Sauce*, peel and mince shallots, garlic and ginger. Slice peppers. Add to hot pan and sauté until softened, about 5 - 8 minutes.

5. Reduce heat to low. Add almond butter, coconut milk, honey, fish sauce, vinegar and lime juice. Whisk until blended. Gently simmer for 10 minutes. Remove from heat, but keep warm.

6. Preheat outdoor grill or griddle pan over medium-high heat. Lightly coat with coconut oil.

7. Pierce marinated chicken strips with soaked skewers. Pour some *Satay Sauce* over chicken and brush lightly with marinade brush to coat. Transfer remaining *Satay Sauce* to serving dish.

8. Grill chicken on preheated grill until just cooked through, about 3 minutes per side. Turn over skewers halfway through cooking. Do not overcook.

9. Remove skewers from heat and transfer to serving dish. Serve with *Satay Sauce*.

Orange Chicken

Prep Time: 10 minutes

Cook Time: 10 minutes

Servings: 2

INGREDIENTS

12 oz (3/4 lb) boneless skinless chicken

1/2 cup almond flour

1 teaspoon flax meal

1 cage-free egg

1 green onion (scallion)

1/4 teaspoon cayenne pepper

1/2 teaspoon paprika

1/2 teaspoon ground black pepper

1/2 teaspoon Celtic sea salt

Coconut oil (for cooking)

Water

Orange Sauce

3 oranges (or tangerines or Clementines)

2 tablespoons raw honey (or agave)

1 tablespoon tamari (or liquid aminos or coconut aminos)

1 small garlic clove

1/2 inch piece fresh ginger

1/4 teaspoon ground black pepper

Water

INSTRUCTIONS

1. For *Orange Sauce*, zest 2 oranges, *then* juice all oranges into small pot. Peel and mince garlic and ginger. Add to pot with honey, tamari and pepper. Add 1/2 cup water.

2. Heat small pot over medium heat and bring to simmer. Simmer until *Orange Sauce* is reduced by half, about 5 minutes. Stir frequently. Remove from heat and set aside.

3. Heat medium pan over medium-high heat. Lightly coat pan with coconut oil.

4. In a shallow dish, blend almond meal, flax meal, salt and spices.

5. Whisk egg and 1 teaspoon water in separate shallow dish.

6. Cut chicken into 1 inch pieces. Dip chicken into egg wash, then dredge in seasoned almond meal.

7. Carefully place coated chicken pieces into hot oil and fry about 2 - 3 minutes, until golden brown and cooked through. Turn with tongs halfway through cooking.

8. Drain cooked chicken on paper towel, then transfer to medium mixing bowl. Pour *Orange Sauce* over chicken and toss to coat. Transfer to serving dish.

9. Slice scallions and sprinkle over dish. Serve hot.

Luscious Zucchini Lasagna

Prep Time: 20 minutes

Cook Time: 40 minutes

Servings: 4

INGREDIENTS

1 large zucchini

Meat Filling

8 oz (1/2 lb) lean ground meat (beef, pork, turkey, chicken, etc.)

1/4 small onion (white, yellow or red)

1 teaspoon dried oregano

1/2 teaspoon garlic powder

1/2 teaspoon dried basil

1/2 teaspoon ground black pepper

1/2 teaspoon Celtic sea salt

Tomato Sauce

6 oz (1 can) organic tomato paste

8 oz (1 can) organic tomato sauce

2 teaspoons dried oregano

1 teaspoon garlic powder

1/2 teaspoon paprika

1/2 teaspoon ground black pepper

1/2 teaspoon Celtic sea salt

Spinach Ricotta

2 cup cashews

1 cup frozen chopped spinach (thawed)

1 teaspoon ground white pepper (or black pepper)

1/2 teaspoon garlic powder

1/2 teaspoon onion powder

1/2 teaspoon dried basil

1/2 teaspoon Celtic sea salt

Water

INSTRUCTIONS

1. *Soak cashews in enough water to cover for at least 4 hours, or overnight in refrigerator. Drain and rinse.

2. Preheat oven to 350 degrees F. Heat medium pan over medium-high heat.

3. For *Meat Filling*, peel onion and grate or mince. Add to hot pan with ground meat, salt and spices. Sauté until meat is browned, about 5 - 8 minutes. Remove from heat and set aside.

4. For *Spinach Ricotta*, add soaked cashews, salt and spices to food processor or high-speed blender. Process until smooth, about 2 minutes. Add chopped spinach and pulse to incorporate. Set aside.

5. For *Pasta Sauce*, add all ingredients to medium mixing bowl and mix until combined. Set aside.

6. Slice zucchini lengthwise into 1/4 inch slices with mandolin or knife.

7. To assemble, layer a few spoonfuls of *Tomato Sauce* along bottom of baking dish. Top with layer of zucchini, *Spinach Ricotta, Meat Filling* and *Sauce*. Repeat process with remaining components.

End with a layer of zucchini, then *Sauce* on top. Add a dash of extra spices, if preferred.

8. Place *Lasagna* in oven and bake for about 40 minutes, until heated through. Remove from oven and let cool about 10 minutes.

9. Serve warm.

Chickplant Filets

Prep time: 10 minutes

Cook time: 50 minutes

Serves: 4

INGREDIENTS

4 grass-fed chicken breasts

1 eggplant

4 pinches fresh basil

¼ tsp chipotle chili pepper powder

¼ tsp curry

1 large carrot

1 red onion

1 cup coconut milk

8 wooden toothpicks

1 tbsp coconut oil

INSTRUCTIONS

1. Cut eggplant into 8 rectangles 3" long by 1" wide and 1" tall. Cut the carrot into matchsticks and dice the onion into small pieces. Cut the chicken in half lengthwise into thin filets. Soak the toothpicks in water. Preheat oven to 350.

2. Combine coconut oil, carrot, onion, 1 tsp curry, basil and chipotle chili pepper powder in a pan over medium heat. Stir together until it forms a sauce. Add eggplant and saute 7-10 minutes or until eggplant is tender.

3. Place 1 slice of eggplant on each of the chicken filets. Drizzle the contents of the pan over each of the filets; roll each fillet up around the eggplant and secure with a toothpick.

4. Place the 8 filets in the oven and bake for 35 minutes.

5. Remove from oven and pour serve 2 filets to each plate. Pour ¼ cup coconut milk and sprinkle curry over each plate's filets. Chill 20 minutes and then serve.

Salmon with Berry Chutney

Prep time: 10 minutes

Cook time: 15 minutes

Serves: 4

INGREDIENTS

4 salmon filets

16 stalks of asparagus

1 cup blueberries

1 onion

1 clove garlic

1 tbsp ginger root

¼ cup apple cider vinegar

½ tsp cinnamon

INSTRUCTIONS

1. Preheat your broiler. Finely chop the onion, garlic and ginger. Prepare a stove-top pot to steam the asparagus.

2. Combine blueberry, onion, garlic, ginger, apple cider vinegar and cinnamon in a saucepan and bring to a simmer, stirring continuously. Remove from heat once it has thickened into a sauce and set aside to cool.

3. Steam the asparagus for 3-5 minutes and broil the fish for 5-7 minutes. Remove from oven.

4. Lay one piece of fish across each plate and pour the blueberry chutney over top. Lay 4 stalks of asparagus over each piece of fish and serve.

Mirepoix with Red Sauce

Prep time: 7 minutes

Cook time: approx. 15 minutes

Serves: 4

INGREDIENTS

Flounder and Mirepoix

4 flounder fillets

1 tbsp extra virgin olive oil

¼ tsp thyme

¼ tsp parsley

1 clove garlic

1 stalk celery

8 baby-cut carrots

1 small onion

¼ cup water

¼ cup clam juice

Roasted Red Pepper sauce

1 tbsp extra virgin olive oil

1/2 small onion

1 clove garlic

¼ tsp smoked paprika

¼ tsp Celtic sea salt

¼ tsp ground white pepper

2 roasted red peppers

3/4 cup organic chicken stock

1 tbsp arrowroot

INSTRUCTIONS

1. For Mirepoix, finely chop the celery, carrots and 1 onion together and place in a bowl.

2. For Roasted Red Pepper sauce, finely chop the ½ onion and combine all the above listed Roasted Red Pepper sauce ingredients together in a pan. Keep warm over very low heat.

3. Combine thyme, parsley and extra virgin olive oil in a braising pan over medium-high heat. Add mirepoix and cook while stirring for 2-3 min until the vegetables are soft but not browned. Add clam juice and Roasted Red Pepper sauce. Season to taste with Celtic sea salt and ground white pepper. Reduce heat to medium-low and simmer 5 min.

4. Season fillets with Celtic sea salt and ground white pepper. Fold the thin end of each fillet underneath itself and place in the pan. Increase heat to a moderate simmer. Cover and poach 5-7 min until internal temperature reaches 130 degrees.

5. Remove fillets from pan and let rest 2 min. Serve immediately afterward, or chill 20 minutes and then serve.

Mushroom Masala

Prep Time: 10 minutes

Cook Time: 25 minutes

Servings: 8

INGREDIENTS

1 head cauliflower

1 1/2 cups tomato purée (or tomato sauce)

1 pint (2 cups) mushrooms

1 onion

1 chili pepper

1/2 green bell pepper

1 large garlic clove

1 inch piece fresh ginger

2 teaspoons coriander leaves (optional)

1 teaspoon garam masala

1/2 teaspoon cayenne pepper

1/2 teaspoon ground coriander

1/2 teaspoon Celtic sea salt

3 tablespoons bacon fat (or coconut oil or ghee)

INSTRUCTIONS

1. Roughly chop cauliflower, then rice cauliflower in food processor, or mince. Add to medium pot with enough water to cover. Heat pot over medium heat and cook until just tender, about 8 minutes. Drain and transfer to serving dish.

2. Heat medium pan over medium heat. Add bacon fat, oil or butter to hot pan.

3. Peel and finely dice onions. Remove seeds, veins and stem from bell pepper and dice. Slice chili pepper. Peel and mince garlic and onion. Add to hot oiled pan and sauté about 5 minutes.

4. Slice mushrooms and add to pan with tomato, salt and spices. Finely chop coriander leaves and add to pan (optional). Sauté and let simmer about 10 - 12 minutes, stirring occasionally.

5. Transfer to serving dish and serve hot with cauliflower rice.

Sweet & Spicy Venison Stir-Fry

Prep Time: 5 minutes*

Cook Time: 10 minutes

Servings: 4

INGREDIENTS

16 oz (1 lb) venison

1 bell pepper (red, yellow or green)

1 small onion (white, red or yellow)

1 small carrot

1/3 cup button mushrooms (about 4 - 5)

2 tablespoons tamari (or coconut aminos or apple cider vinegar)

1 teaspoon raw honey (or agave or date butter)

1 garlic clove

1/2 inch piece fresh ginger

1/4 teaspoon allspice (optional)

1/2 teaspoon red pepper flakes

1 teaspoon ground black pepper

1 1/2 teaspoons Celtic sea salt

3 tablespoons coconut oil

INSTRUCTIONS

1. *Peel and mince garlic. Cut venison into 1/2 inch strips. Add to medium mixing bowl with 1 tablespoon coconut oil, and 1/2 of salt and spices. Mix to combine. Set aside in refrigerator at least 30 minutes.

2. Heat large pan or skillet over medium heat. Add 1 tablespoon coconut oil to hot pan.

3. Remove stem, seeds and veins from bell pepper. Peel onion. Slice pepper, onion, carrot and mushrooms. Peel and mince or grate ginger. Add to medium mixing bowl with remaining salt and spices.

4. Add seasoned veggies to hot oiled pan. Sauté until tender and lightly browned, about 2 minutes.

5. Add remaining coconut oil, tamari and honey to pan. Add marinated venison and sauté until just cooked, about 2 - 3 minutes.

6. Transfer to serving dish and serve hot.

Herb Roasted Pork Tenderloin

Prep Time: 10 minutes*

Cook Time: 15 minutes

Servings: 4

INGREDIENTS

1 pork tenderloin

1 teaspoon dried rosemary

1 teaspoon dried thyme

1 teaspoon dried oregano

1 teaspoon dried basil

1 teaspoon dried marjoram (optional)

1/2 teaspoon ground black pepper

1 teaspoon Celtic sea salt

Apricot Sauce

1 cup dried apricots

2/3 cup water

1 teaspoon apple cider vinegar (or dry white wine)

INSTRUCTIONS

1. Preheat oven to 425 degrees F. Heat small pan over medium heat.

2. Rub tenderloin with salt and spices, then press into meat so it
    adheres. Place on sheet pan, or wire rack over sheet pan.

3. Roast for 10 - 15 minutes, until just cooked through and no pink
    remains. Remove pork from oven and let rest 10 minutes.

4. For *Apricot Sauce*, add dried apricots, water and vinegar to food processor or high-speed blender. Process until smooth, about 1 - 2 minutes.

5. Add *Apricot Sauce* to hot pan and reduce until slightly thickened. Stir well and do not let burn. Remove from heat.

6. Slice pork and transfer to serving dish. Top pork with *Apricot Sauce* and serve warm.

Ground Beef Stuffed Peppers

Prep Time: 10 minutes

Cook Time: 50 minutes

Servings: 4

INGREDIENTS

4 bell peppers

16 oz (1 lb) ground meat (beef, pork, chicken, turkey, etc.)

1/2 head cauliflower (1 cup riced)

1/2 cup roasted red peppers

1/4 cup sundried tomatoes

1/4 cup pecans

1/2 small onion (white, yellow or red)

2 tablespoons coconut oil

2 garlic cloves

Medium bunch fresh herbs (parsley, oregano, thyme, etc.)

1/4 teaspoon red pepper flakes

1 teaspoon ground white pepper (or black pepper)

1 teaspoon Celtic sea salt

Water

INSTRUCTIONS

1. Preheat oven to 350 degrees F.
2. Cut tops off peppers, then remove stems from tops and seeds and veins from bottoms of peppers. Leave bottoms of peppers hollow

but do not pierce. Place in baking dish just large enough to fit peppers snuggly. Set aside.

3. Peel onion and garlic. Roughly chop onions, garlic and cauliflower. Add to food processor or high-speed blender with pecans. Pulse about 15 seconds.

4. Add tops of peppers, roasted red peppers, sundried tomatoes, ground meat, salt, pepper, and fresh herbs to processor. Process until coarsely ground, about 1 - 2 minutes.

5. Use large spoon to stuff peppers with mixture. Add 1/2 cup water to bottom of baking dish. Cover peppers with aluminum foil.

6. Bake 30 minutes. Carefully remove foil and continue baking uncovered 10 - 20 minutes, until stuffing is golden brown and cooked through .

7. Carefully remove from oven and transfer peppers to serving dish. Serve hot.

Healthy Gyro with Creamy Tzatziki

Prep Time: 10 minutes

Cook Time: 30 minutes

Servings: 2

INGREDIENTS

2 large romaine lettuce leaves

1 tomato

1/2 small red onion

Gyro Meat

8 oz (1/2 lb) ground lamb

8 oz (1/2 lb) ground beef

1 small onion (white or yellow)

2 garlic cloves

1 teaspoon dried marjoram

1 teaspoon dried oregano

1 teaspoon dried rosemary

1 teaspoon ground black pepper

1 teaspoon Celtic sea salt

Coconut oil (for cooking)

Coconut Cream Tzatziki

1/2 small cucumber

1/4 cup coconut cream (settled from full-fat canned coconut milk)

1 teaspoon lemon juice

1/2 teaspoon apple cider vinegar

2 mint leaves

1 sprig fresh dill

1 garlic clove

1/4 teaspoon Celtic sea salt

INSTRUCTIONS

1. Preheat oven to 325 degrees F. Line small loaf pan with parchment or aluminum foil.

2. For *Gyro Meat*, peel white or yellow onion and add to food processor or high-speed blender. Process until finely ground, about 30 seconds. Turn out onto cheesecloth or paper towels. Squeeze or compress onions to remove as much liquid as possible.

3. Add drained onions back to processor. Peel garlic and add to processor with lamb, beef, herbs, salt and pepper. Process until mixture is smooth, about 2 - 3 minutes. Scrape down sides of bowl as necessary.

4. Add mixture to prepared loaf pan. Pack tightly and smooth top. Bake for 30 minutes. Remove from oven and allow to rest about 5 minutes.

5. For *Coconut Cream Tzatziki*, peel, seed and shred, grate or dice cucumber. Peel and mince garlic. Mince mint and dill. Add to small mixing bowl with coconut cream, lemon juice, salt and vinegar. Mix well, then set aside to chill in refrigerator.

6. Heat medium skillet over medium-high heat and lightly coat with coconut oil.

7. Carefully release *Gyro Meat* from loaf pan and peel away parchment or aluminum. Use tongs and sharp knife to cut lengthwise into 1/4 inch thick slices.

8. Add sliced meat to hot oiled skillet in single layer and sear about 2 minutes on each side, until browned and lightly crisp. Flip halfway through cooking.

9. Peel and slice red onion. Seed and chop tomato. Transfer romaine lettuce to serving dishes. Layer *Gyro Meat* over lettuce, then top with *Coconut Cream Tzatziki*, onions and tomatoes.

10. Use lettuce to wrap up meat and veggies and serve immediately.

Chicken Souvlaki Kebobs

Prep Time: 5 minutes*

Cook Time: 15 minutes

Servings: 4

INGREDIENTS

12 oz (3/4 lb) boneless skinless chicken

1 lemon

2 garlic cloves

1/2 small white onion

1/2 yellow bell pepper

1/2 cup grape tomato

1 teaspoon dried oregano

3/4 teaspoon Celtic sea salt

2 tablespoons coconut oil

8 skewers

INSTRUCTIONS

1. *Soak wooden skewers in water for 10 minutes, if using.
2. Juice lemon into medium mixing bowl. Peel and mince garlic. Remove stem, seeds and veins from bell pepper. Peel onion. Roughly chop pepper and onion. Add to bowl with tomatoes, 1 tablespoon coconut oil, oregano and salt.
3. *Pierce chicken multiple times with fork, then cut into one inch chunks. Add to bowl and mix to combine. Let set aside in refrigerator for 10 minutes.

4. Heat small skillet or griddle over medium-high heat and add 1 tablespoon coconut oil.
5. Drain marinated chicken and veggies, then carefully add to skewer, alternating meat and veggies.
6. Add chicken and veggie skewer to hot oiled skillet or griddle. Grill for about 1 - 2 minutes then turn 1/4 the way around. Continue cooking and turning until chicken is golden brown and cooked through.
7. Remove from heat and serve immediately.

Stuffed Cabbage in Tomato Sauce

Prep Time: 15 minutes

Cook Time: 60 minutes

Servings: 6

INGREDIENTS

1 large cabbage head

Filling

2 1/2 lbs ground beef

4 cage-free eggs

1/2 onion (yellow or white)

1/3 cup almond flour

1/2 cup cauliflower (riced or minced)

1/2 teaspoon dried thyme

1/2 teaspoon ground black pepper (or ground white pepper)

1 1/2 teaspoons Celtic sea salt

Tomato Sauce

2 cans (15 oz) organic tomato sauce

1/2 cup golden raisins

1/2 onion (yellow or white)

2 tablespoons raw honey (or agave or date butter)

2 tablespoons apple cider vinegar

1 1/2 teaspoons Celtic sea salt

1 teaspoon ground black pepper (or ground white pepper)

2 tablespoons bacon fat (or coconut oil or ghee)

INSTRUCTIONS

1. Preheat oven to 350 degrees F. Bring large pot of salted water to boil.

2. Carefully place cabbage head in boiling water for about 5 minutes. Use tongs to peel each layer of leaves from head as soon as they become tender. Set leaves aside on sheet pan to cool.

3. For *Tomato Sauce*, peel and mince onions. Add 1/2 of onions to medium mixing bowl. Add tomato sauce, honey, vinegar, raisins, salt and spices and mix to combine.

4. For *Filling*, add remaining onions to large mixing bowl. Mince or rice cauliflower and add to bowl with eggs, almond flour, salt, spices, and 1 cup *Tomato Sauce.* Mix well with hands or large wooden spoon.

5. Cut hard rib from bottom of each cooled cabbage leaf. Place 1/3 - 1/2 cup *Filling* near the bottom edge of cabbage leaf and roll into a neat package, tucking in sides as you roll. Repeat with remaining filling and cabbage.

6. Spread 1 cup *Tomato sauce* along bottom of deep, lidded baking dish. Place 1/2 the cabbage rolls in baking dish. Add 1/2 remaining sauce, the remaining cabbage rolls. Top with remaining sauce.

7. Tightly cover dish with lid and bake for 1 hour, until meat is cooked through and veggies are tender.

8. Transfer to serving dish and serve hot.

Slow Cooker Herbed Duck

Prep Time: 10 minutes

Cook Time: 4 hours

Servings: 4

INGREDIENTS

5 lb whole duck (innards removed)

2 cups chicken stock (or broth)

1/2 cup dry white wine (or 1/4 cup apple cider vinegar + 1/4 cup apple juice)

1 1/2 cups pitted French green olives

2 onions (yellow or white)

1 large celery stalk

1 tablespoon raw honey (or agave)

1 tablespoon organic tomato paste

8 cloves garlic

2 bay leaves

2 sprigs fresh rosemary

1 teaspoon dried thyme

1 teaspoon dried basil

1 teaspoon dried parsley

1 tablespoon dried oregano

1/2 teaspoon ground black pepper

1 teaspoon Celtic sea salt

1 teaspoon dried lavender buds (food grade) (optional)

1 teaspoon dried marjoram (optional)

1 teaspoon fennel seed (optional)

1/2 teaspoon dried tarragon(optional)

1 small bunch flat-leaf Italian parsley (optional)

INSTRUCTIONS

1. Rub tomato paste, honey, salt and spices into duck, over an under skin where possible.
2. Peel onions. Roughly chop 1 onion and celery, then stuff into duck cavity. Set aside in slow cooker.
3. Slice remaining onions. Add to slow cooker with chicken stock and white wine.
4. Cover slow cooker with lid. Turn on to high and cook 4 - 5 hours, until meat is cooked through.
5. Turn off slow cooker and carefully remove lid. Carve duck and transfer to serving dish.
6. Serve hot.

Jamaican Curried Goat

Prep Time: 30 minutes*

Cook Time: 5 hours

Servings: 6

INGREDIENTS

3 lb goat or lamb (boneless or bone-in)

2 cans (14 oz) full-fat coconut milk

1 can (15 oz) organic tomato sauce (or crushed tomatoes)

5 large parsnips

2 onions (yellow or white)

1 chili pepper (habañero, scotch bonnet, etc.)

2 inch piece fresh ginger

4 garlic cloves

6 tablespoons Jamaican curry powder (or 6 tablespoons curry powder + 1 tablespoon allspice)

1 tablespoon dried thyme

1 tablespoon Celtic sea salt

1/4 cup coconut oil (for cooking)

1 - 2 cups water

INSTRUCTIONS

1. *Season goat with salt and set aside in baking dish until room temperature, about up to 30 minutes.

2. Heat large skillet over medium-high heat. Add coconut oil to hot pan.

3. Peel and chop onions. Peel and mince garlic and ginger. Remove stem and seeds from chili pepper, then finely chop. Cut goat into chunks.

4. Add 2 tablespoon curry powder to hot oil. Add goat to hot seasoned oil in batches to brown, about 5 minutes per batch. Set aside in slow cooker.

5. Add onions and chili pepper to hot pan. Sauté until just golden and fragrant, about 5 - 8 minutes. Add garlic and ginger. Sauté about 1 minute.

6. Add onion mixture and remaining curry powder to slow cooker. Add tomato sauce, coconut milk and water. Stir to combine.

7. Cover slow cooker with lid. Turn on to high and cook about 4 hours, until just tender but not done.

8. Roughly chop parsnips and add to slow cooker. Cover with liquid. Continue cooking about 1 hour, until meat and veggies are tender.

9. Turn off slow cooker and carefully remove lid. Skim off any fat from surface and remove any bones.

10. Transfer to serving dish and serve hot.

Basque Style Cod Fish Stew

Prep Time: 30 minutes*

Cook Time: 45 minutes

Servings: 4

INGREDIENTS

8 oz (1/2 lb) salted cod fish

1/2 cup tomato sauce

1/4 cup white wine (or 3 tablespoons white grape juice + 1 tablespoon apple cider vinegar)

2 cage-free eggs

2 large parsnips

1 onion (yellow, red or white)

1 large garlic clove

1/4 cup golden raisins

2 oz roasted red bell peppers (jarred)

2 tablespoons green olives (pitted)

1 teaspoon capers

1 bay leaf

1/4 cup coconut oil

Water

INSTRUCTIONS

1. *Soak salted cod in 2 quarts of water for 8 hours. Change water 3 times throughout soaking time. Drain and cut fish into chunks.

2. Bring small pot of salted water to boil. Hard boil eggs about 10 minutes. Drain and set aside in cold water to cool. Crack and peel shells.

3. Peel onion and garlic. Mince garlic. Slice onion, parsnips, and cooled eggs.

4. In order, layer half of parsnips, cod, onion, eggs, capers, garlic, olives, peppers and raisins in medium pot. Add bay leaf, then half of tomato sauce and coconut oil.

5. In order, layer remaining parsnips, cod, onion, eggs, capers, garlic, olives, peppers and raisins. Add 1 cup water and wine on top. Do not stir.

6. Heat pot over medium heat, cover and bring to a boil. Reduce heat to medium-low and simmer until parsnips are tender, about 30 minutes.

7. Transfer to sourcing dishes and serve immediately.

Indian Lamb Stew

Prep Time: 15 minutes

Cook Time: 2 hours 30 minutes

Servings: 4

INGREDIENTS

32 oz (1 lb) stew lamb (or lamb shank)

3 cups beef stock (or vegetable or chicken stock)

2 tablespoons tapioca flour (or arrowroot powder)

2 large carrots

2 large celery stalks

2 large parsnips

2 medium tomatoes

1 green bell pepper

1 red bell pepper

1 small onion (yellow, white or red)

4 garlic cloves

1 inch piece fresh ginger

3 tablespoons curry powder

1 tablespoon ground coriander

1 tablespoon ground cumin

2 teaspoons ground cinnamon

2 teaspoons black pepper

1 teaspoon ground cardamom (optional)

Celtic sea salt, to taste

2 tablespoons coconut oil

Water

INSTRUCTIONS

1. Heat large pot over medium heat. Add coconut oil to hot pot.
2. Add lamb to hot oiled pot. Sauté about 10 minutes, turning occasionally to brown on all sides.
3. Peel onion. Remove stems, seeds and veins from bell peppers. Roughly chop onion, bell pepper, carrots, celery, and tomato.
4. Peel and mince garlic and ginger. Add to pot and sauté until fragrant, about 2 minutes.
5. Add veggies to pot with tapioca, spices and salt, to taste. Stir to combine.
6. Add stock or broth to pot, plus enough water to immerse meat and veggies. Bring to simmer, then reduce heat to low.
7. Place lid loosely over pot to prevent splatter. Let simmer about 1 hour.
8. Remove lid and stir. Add water if necessary to prevent burning. Replace lid and continuing cooking another hour.
9. Remove lid and stir. Remove lamb from pot and cut meat from bone, if using bone-in lamb. Chop meat and place back into pot. Stir to combine.
10. Transfer to serving dish and serve hot.

Macadamia Crusted Ahi Tuna

Prep Time: 5 minutes

Cook Time: 1 minute

Servings: 1

INGREDIENTS

8 oz ahi tuna fillet

1/4 teaspoon coconut oil

1/4 teaspoon dried thyme

1/4 teaspoon dried tarragon (optional)

1/4 cup whole macadamia nuts (shelled)

1 small garlic clove teaspoon

1 small shallot teaspoon

1/2 teaspoon ground white pepper (or black pepper)

1/2 teaspoon sea salt

2 tablespoons coconut oil

INSTRUCTIONS

1. Heat medium pan over medium-high heat. Add 2 tablespoons coconut oil to pan.
2. Chop macadamia nuts well. Peel and finely mince garlic and shallot. Set aside.
3. Rub top and bottom of fillet with 1/4 teaspoon coconut oil, salt, pepper, thyme and tarragon (optional).
4. Press 1/2 chopped macadamia nuts into each side of fillet.

5. Add garlic and shallots to hot oiled pan and sauté for just a second. Do not burn.

6. Carefully place fish in pan and sear 15 - 30 seconds on each side, for rare to medium rare. Carefully flip half way through cooking.

7. Transfer fillet to serving dish and serve hot with mixed greens or favorite veggies.

Cashew Crunch Kelp Noodle Salad

Prep Time: 10 minutes*

Servings: 2

INGREDIENTS

1 package (12 oz) kelp noodles

1/2 lemon

1/2 small red bell pepper

Cashew Sauce

1 cup raw cashews

1/2 small red bell pepper

1/2 lemon

1 tablespoon coconut aminos (or raw apple cider vinegar)

2 large basil leaves

1/2 teaspoon smoked paprika

1/2 teaspoon ground black pepper

1/2 teaspoon Celtic sea salt

1/4 teaspoon ground turmeric (optional)

1/4 teaspoon smoked chili powder (optional)

Water

INSTRUCTIONS

1. *Soak 3/4 cup cashews in enough water to cover at least 4 hours, or overnight in refrigerator. Drain and rinse.

2. Drain and rinse kelp noodles. Add to medium bowl with warm water and juice of 1/2 lemon. Set aside 5 minutes.

3. Cut bell pepper in half. Remove stem, seeds and veins and set half of pepper aside. Julienne (thinly slice) remaining bell pepper and add to medium mixing bowl.

1. For *Crunchy Cashew Sauce*, add soaked cashews, bell pepper, juice of 1/2 lemon, coconut aminos, basil, salt and spices to food processor or high-speed blender. Process until smooth, about 2 minutes. Add enough water to reach desired consistency. Set aside.

4. Drain kelp noodles and add to sliced bell pepper. Add *Cashew Sauce* and toss to coat. Transfer noodles to serving dishes.

5. Roughly chop remaining 1/4 cup cashews. Sprinkle noodles and serve immediately. Or refrigerate for 20 minutes and serve chilled.

Tuna Tartar with Avocado and Mango

Prep Time: 15 minutes

Servings: 2

INGREDIENTS

8 oz tuna steak (sushi grade)

1 mango

1 avocado

1 lime

1 garlic clove

Small bunch fresh cilantro

2 tablespoons raw oil (sesame, coconut, almond, walnut, etc.)

1 teaspoon coconut aminos (or raw apple cider vinegar)

1/4 teaspoon red pepper flake

1/4 teaspoon Celtic sea salt

1/4 teaspoon ground pepper

2 tablespoons raw macadamia nuts (optional)

INSTRUCTIONS

1. Add oil, coconut aminos and red pepper flake in small bowl. Cut lime in half and add squeeze of lime. Mix to combine and set aside.

2. Cut avocado in half and remove pit. Dice flesh in peel and scoop into small mixing bowl. Finely chop cilantro. Add to medium mixing bowl with squeeze of remaining lime, salt and pepper. Mix to combine, then set aside.

3. Peel garlic and mince. Cut mango in half around pit. Peel and dice. Add to separate mixing bowl with 1 tablespoon oil and pepper mixture. Toss to coat. Set aside.

4. Dice tuna, discarding any tough white gristle. Finely chop macadamia nuts.

5. Transfer tuna to serving dish. Place in ring mold to form, if preferred. Top with mango and avocado mixtures. Sprinkle on chopped nuts. Drizzle on remaining oil and pepper mixture if preferred.

6. Serve immediately. Or refrigerate 20 minutes and serve chilled.

Dill Stuffed Tomatoes

Prep Time: 15 minutes*

Servings: 2

INGREDIENTS

4 medium tomatoes

1 celery stalk

1 small carrot

1 green onion (scallion)

1/3 cup sunflower seeds

1/2 red bell pepper

1/4 small red onion (or sweet onion)

1/2 teaspoon Celtic sea salt

Dill Dressing

1/2 cup raw cashews

1 tablespoon raw apple cider vinegar (or coconut aminos)

1 teaspoon ground mustard (or mustard seeds)

1/2 lemon

1 small garlic clove

2 sprigs fresh dill

1/2 teaspoon Celtic sea salt

1/4 teaspoon ground white pepper (or pinch ground black pepper)

Water

INSTRUCTIONS

1. *Soak cashews in enough water to cover at least 4 hours, or overnight in refrigerator. Drain and rinse.

2. Cut tops off tomatoes and scoop out seeds. Set aside.

3. Finely dice celery and carrot. Slice green onion. Peel and dice onion. Add to medium mixing bowl. Remove stem, seeds and veins from bell pepper, then dice. Add to bowl with sprinkle of salt. Set aside.

4. For *Dill Dressing*, peel garlic and add to food processor or high-speed blender with soaked cashews, vinegar, mustard, squeeze of lemon, dill, salt and pepper. Process until smooth and creamy, about 1 - 2 minutes. Add enough water to reach desired consistency.

5. Pour *Dill Dressing* over chopped veggies. Toss to coat.

6. Plate hollowed tomatoes and stuff with *Dill Dressing* veggie mixture. Serve immediately.

Cod with Saffron and Garlic

Prep Time: 5 minutes

Cook Time: 15 minutes

Servings: 2

INGREDIENTS

1 pound fresh cod fillets

2 Tablespoons olive oil

4 garlic cloves, thinly sliced

1 shallot, thinly sliced

Pinch of saffron threads

1 Tablespoon lemon juice

½ teaspoon dried parsley

Lemon wedges for serving (optional)

1 teaspoon sea salt

INSTRUCTIONS

1. In a skillet, sauté the garlic and shallots in oil until translucent.
2. Add the fish to the skillet.
3. Mix the saffron, lemon juice, parsley, and salt in a small bowl and pour over the fish.
4. Cover the skillet and cook on low heat for about 10 minutes, until fish is opaque and flakes easily.
5. Serve with lemon wedges.

Turkey Cutlets

Prep Time: 5 minutes

Cook Time: 20 minutes

Servings: 4

INGREDIENTS

2 pounds sliced raw turkey cutlets

4 Tablespoons olive oil

2 garlic cloves, sliced

1 cup chicken broth

1 Tablespoon lemon juice

2 Tablespoons capers

¼ cup fresh parsley, chopped.

½ teaspoon sea salt

INSTRUCTIONS

1. Heat turkey in 3 Tablespoons oil in a heavy skillet over high heat. Cook the turkey until brown on both sides and cooked through, about 3 minutes per side. Transfer turkey to a plate, and cover to keep warm.

2. Add remaining oil to the skillet and sauté the garlic. Add the broth and cook over medium-high heat, until reduced to about ¾ cup. Stir in lemon juice, capers, parsley, and sea salt.

3. Return the turkey to the skillet and cook until heated through, about 1-2 minutes.

Sweet Potato Shepherd's Pie

Prep Time: 10 minutes

Cook Time: 50 minutes

Servings: 4

INGREDIENTS

1 pound ground turkey

1 large onion, chopped

2 medium zucchini, chopped

2 large sweet potatoes, peeled and diced

1 teaspoon dried thyme

1 teaspoon dried basil

2 Tablespoons olive oil

1 teaspoon sea salt

INSTRUCTIONS

1. Brown the meat with the onion in a large skillet. Cook until meat is fully cooked, about 15-20 minutes.
2. In another stockpot, steam sweet potatoes for about 20 minutes.
3. Add the zucchini and spices to the meat and cook for another 5 minutes.
4. Preheat oven to 400 °F.
5. Drain the sweet potatoes and return them to the pot. Mash with a potato masher and mix in the olive oil and sea salt.
6. Transfer the meat to a large casserole pan and pat it down with a spatula.

7. Spoon the mashed sweet potatoes on top of the meat, and spread it evenly across the pan.

8. Bake for 30 minutes.

Beef & Mushroom Casserole

Prep Time: 15 minutes

Cook Time: 1 hour and 20 minutes

Servings: 4

INGREDIENTS

2 pounds ground beef

1 pound mushrooms, washed and halved

1 onion, chopped

1 large head cauliflower, chopped

1/2 cup beef stock

2 Tablespoons olive oil

1 teaspoon dried parsley

1 teaspoon dried marjoram

1 teaspoon dried rosemary

1 teaspoon sea salt

INSTRUCTIONS

1. Brown the meat with the onion, celery, carrots, mushrooms, and garlic in a large stockpot. Cook until meat is fully cooked, about 15-20 minutes. Add the beef stock, rosemary, and thyme and stir.
2. In another stockpot, steam cauliflower for about 20 minutes.
3. Preheat oven to 400 °F.
4. Drain the cauliflower and return it to the pot. Mash it with a potato masher. Mix in the olive oil and sea salt.
5. Transfer the beef mixture to a large casserole pan and pat down with a spatula.

6. Spread the mashed cauliflower over the top of the meat.

7. Sprinkle the parsley on top of the casserole and put it in the oven.

8. Bake for 40 minutes, until cauliflower starts to brown.

Sweet and Sour Chicken

Prep Time: 10 minutes

Cook Time: 20 minutes

Servings: 4

INGREDIENTS

1 pound skinless chicken breasts, cut into cubes

1 bunch scallions, chopped

1 cup pineapple, chopped (fresh or frozen)

2 large carrots, thinly sliced

2 stalks celery, sliced

½ pound mushrooms, halved

¼ cup apple cider vinegar

2 tablespoons coconut oil

1-inch piece of ginger, peeled and minced

2 cloves garlic, minced

INSTRUCTIONS

1. In a large skillet or walk, sauté the onions, celery, and garlic in the oil until soft, about 2 minutes.
2. Add the carrots, the mushrooms, the pineapple, and the chicken and continue stir-frying another 5 minutes.
3. Add the vinegar, cover, and reduce heat to low for 10 minutes.

Roasted Turkey Legs

Prep Time: 5 minutes

Cook Time: 50 minutes

Servings: 4

INGREDIENTS

4 turkey legs

4 Tablespoons coconut oil, melted

2 Tablespoons apple cider vinegar

1 teaspoon ground ginger

1 teaspoon ground cinnamon

1 teaspoon turmeric

1 teaspoon garlic powder

1 teaspoon sea salt

INSTRUCTIONS

1. Preheat oven to 400 °F.
2. In a small bowl, whisk together the oil, vinegar, spices, and salt.
3. Place turkey on a baking sheet and brush each leg with the oil and spice mixture. Do not discard the remaining sauce.
4. Roast the turkey for 20 minutes.
5. Remove from the oven, brush with the remaining sauce, lower the heat to 300 °F and cook for another 30 minutes.

Black Pepper Stew

Prep time: 15 minutes

Cook time: 3 hr 45 minutes

Serves: 6

INGREDIENTS

1 ½ lbs beef stew meat

1 onion

1 (14.5 oz) can no-salt added stewed tomatoes, undrained

¼ tsp Celtic sea salt

½ tsp ground black pepper

1 dried bay leaf

2 cups water

3 tbsp arrowroot powder

12 small sweet potatoes cut in half

30 baby-cut carrots

INSTRUCTIONS

1. Heat oven to 325 degrees. In a bowl, mix arrowroot in water and stir to a paste (if you're not using arrowroot, use 1 cup water instead). Cut the onion into 8 wedges and cut potatoes in half.

2. In ovenproof Dutch oven, mix beef, onion, tomatoes, Celtic sea salt, ground black pepper and bay leaf. Mix arrowroot-thickened water (or 1 cup water) into Dutch oven.

3. Cover and bake for 2 hours, stirring one time.

4. Stir in the potatoes and carrots. Cover and bake until beef and vegetables are tender, about 1 hr 45 min. Remove bay leaf and serve immediately, or chill 20 minutes and then serve.

Spicy Kale Quiche

Prep time: 10 minutes

Cook time: 15 minutes

Serves: 4

INGREDIENTS

8 cage-free eggs

2 tbsp extra virgin olive oil

1 7oz bag of Kale greens

1 shallot

¼ tsp chipotle chili pepper powder

2 cloves garlic

½ lemon

2 tbsp coconut oil

¼ tbsp ground black pepper

INSTRUCTIONS
1. Place a steamer basket in the bottom of a large pot and fill with water; if you see water rise above the bottom of the basket, pour some out. Bring the water to a boil.
2. Wash the kale and remove the stems. Mince the garlic and shallot and squeeze the juice from the lemon into a bowl.
3. In a large pan, add the eggs and extra virgin olive oil. Mixing in the chipotle chili pepper powder, scramble the eggs, breaking them up until they form many small pieces, tender yet firm.
4. Place the kale in the pot and steam until tender and bright-green.

5. Remove the kale from the pot and combine with the eggs. Add the garlic, shallot and lemon juice, drizzle the coconut oil over top and add the ground black pepper. Mix and stir thoroughly.

6. Serve immediately or chill 20 minutes and then serve.

Red Pepper Chicken Fries

Prep time: 10 minutes

Cook time: 12 minutes

Serves: 4

INGREDIENTS

4 pieces grass-fed chicken thighs

1 large red pepper

1 large yellow pepper

1 large orange pepper

1 onion

1 clove garlic

1 tbsp coconut oil

¼ tsp ground black pepper

¼ tsp chinese five spice

INSTRUCTIONS

1. Chop the chicken into small cubes, about 1" each. Chop the peppers and onion into ½" cubes. Mince garlic.
2. In a pan, combine coconut oil with peppers and onion and cook over medium heat for 4 minutes.
3. Add chicken, pepper, chinese five spice, and stir, cooking 4 more minutes.

4. Flip and mix well (in order to cook chicken evenly), add garlic, and cook for 4 more minutes, or until chicken is cooked through.

5. Serve immediately or chill 20 minutes and then serve.

Nuts & Turkey Burgers

Prep time: 10 minutes

Cook time: 6-12 minutes

Servings: 4

INGREDIENTS

16 oz ground turkey

1 cup walnuts

2 cloves garlic

1 onion

¼ tsp chipotle chili pepper powder

¼ tbsp smoked paprika

¼ tsp ground black pepper

INSTRUCTIONS

1. Chop walnuts into smaller pieces, about ⅛" cubes. Mince garlic and chop onion into small pieces, about ¼" pieces.
2. Combine the above with ground turkey and add chipotle chili pepper powder, smoked paprika and ground black pepper. Knead it all together and separate into four patties.
3. Cook on the grill on high heat, flipping occasionally, until desired done-ness.

Chicken Bruschetta

Prep time: 10 minutes

Cook time: 10 minutes

Serves: 4

INGREDIENTS

4 grass-fed chicken breasts

2 tomatoes

4 olives

2 onions

¼ tsp ground black pepper

1 cup roasted red pepper

3 tbsp extra virgin olive oil

INSTRUCTIONS

1. Dice the tomatoes, chop the olives and onions, and combine them with ground black pepper and 2 tbsp olive oil in a bowl and mix well into a bruschetta. Puree the roasted red pepper in a blender and set aside.
2. Combine the chicken with 1 tbsp extra virgin olive oil and cook in a pan over medium-high heat for 4 minutes, turn once, and cook another 4-6 minutes, removing from heat while still tender.
3. Place one piece of chicken on each plate and pour the roasted red pepper over each, adding bruschetta over the top. Garnish with basil and serve.

Spicy Zucchini Eggplant Dine

Prep time: 15 minutes

Cook time: 20 minutes

Serves: 4

INGREDIENTS

3 small zucchini

1 eggplant

2 green peppers

6 tomatoes

1 onion

2 medium carrots

1 four-inch sweet orange pepper

1 cup water

1 tbsp extra virgin olive oil

INSTRUCTIONS

1. Using a julienne peeler, peel zucchini, eggplant and green peppers. Green peppers may be too tough for a julienne peeler, in which case try to simulate the effect of one using a knife. Combine the above in a pan with extra virgin olive oil and saute over medium heat, stirring, for 5 minutes.

2. Meanwhile, cut tomatoes into quarters, carrots into ½" thick slices, dice sweet pepper and dice onion. In a saucepan, combine the above with water and cook over medium heat until carrot is tender,

about 15 minutes. Once finished, blend using an immersion blender, or pour into a blender and puree.

3. Pour the sauce over the zucchini, eggplant and peppers and serve.

Baked Tilapia Filets

Prep time: 10 minutes

Cook time: 15 minutes

Serves: 4

INGREDIENTS

4 filets of tilapia

¼ tsp chipotle chili pepper powder

1 lemon

1 cup coconut milk

1 clove garlic

1 tsp lemon juice

2 tbsp dill

¼ tsp black ground pepper

INSTRUCTIONS

1. Preheat oven to 350 degrees. Chop the garlic and the dill and cut the lemon into slices.
2. Season tilapia with chipotle chili pepper powder and black ground pepper. Bake for 15 minutes or until tilapia flakes with a fork.
3. Combine coconut milk, garlic, lemon juice and dill in a bowl.
4. Remove fish from oven and pour sauce over the top, placing a lemon wedge over each. Serve immediately or chill 20 minutes and then serve.

Red Pepper with Chicken Toppings

Prep time: 15 minutes

Cook time: 15 minutes

Serves: 2

INGREDIENTS

Pizza

1 red pepper

1 yellow pepper

1 small red onion

1 low-sodium cooked organic grass-fed chicken sausage link

1 cup broccoli florets

1 tbsp extra virgin olive oil

Pesto

1 packed cup fresh basil

¼ cup extra virgin olive oil

¼ cup walnuts

3 cloves garlic

¼ tsp Celtic sea salt

¼ tsp ground black pepper

INSTRUCTIONS

1. Cut the peppers in half. Remove the stems, cores and seeds. Line a baking sheet with aluminum foil and place the peppers in it skin

side up. Put peppers under the broiler and leave them there until the skin has begun to turn black and shriveled.

2. Remove peppers from oven, place in a plastic bag and place in refrigerator until cool.

3. Peel the skins off the peppers and throw them away.

4. Slice the onion into half moon slices and slice the chicken sausage link into twelve thin slices. Place the onion, sausage slices and broccoli florets with 1 tbsp extra virgin olive oil in a saucepan over medium heat for 4 minutes until vegetables are tender crisp and meat is slightly browned.

5. Place all the pesto ingredients in a food processor and blend until smooth.

6. Put two halves of roasted pepper on a dish, one red and one yellow, open side up. Using a spoon, spread pesto evenly inside each pepper half. Evenly distribute broccoli, onion, and sausage over the tops.

7. Serve.

Natural Italian Chicken Sausage

Prep Time: 5 minutes

Cook Time: 10 minutes

Servings: 4

INGREDIENTS

20 oz (1 1/4 lb) chicken (ground meat or whole pieces)

1/2 teaspoon all spice

1 teaspoon fennel seed

1 teaspoon ground sage

1 teaspoon dried thyme

1 teaspoon ground black pepper

1 teaspoon Celtic sea salt

Natural or synthetic sausage casing (optional)

Piping or kitchen bag (optional)

Coconut oil (for cooking)

INSTRUCTIONS

1. Heat medium skillet over medium heat and lightly coat with coconut oil.
2. Remove chicken skin and bones from pieces and coarsely grind in food processor, high-speed blender or meat grinder, if using.
3. Add ground chicken to medium mixing bowl with salt and spices and mix well.
4. Use meat grinder to stuff mixture into casing. Or scoop mixture into piping bag with no tip or kitchen bag with 1 inch corner cut

off, and pipe into casing. Twist casing tightly in opposite directions to section off 4-inch links while stuffing.

5.   Or form into 8 - 12 round patties with hands.

6.   Place links or patties in hot oiled skillet. Cook links about 4 - 5 minutes per side, until golden brown and cooked through. Or cook patties about 3 - 4 minutes per side, until golden brown and crisp. Turn halfway through cooking.

7.   Drain cooked sausage on paper towel. Serve hot.

Made in the USA
San Bernardino, CA
08 November 2014